The Modern Guide to Finding, Measuring, and Scaling **Product Market Fit**

GROWTH DATA ANALYTICS PLAYBOOK

Mengying Li   Joe Kumar   Yuzheng Sun

STATSIG

GROWTH DATA ANALYTICS PLAYBOOK
The Modern Guide to Finding, Measuring, and Scaling Product-Market Fit

FIRST EDITION

ISBN   978-1-5445-4983-5   *Hardcover*
       978-1-5445-4982-8   *Paperback*
       978-1-5445-4984-2   *Ebook*

CONTENTS

INTRODUCTION

WHO THIS BOOK IS FOR

The *Growth Data Analytics Playbook* is intended for anyone with an interest in growth data analytics.

- Data analysts, data scientists, and product growth analysts can directly apply the frameworks and models in this book to their daily work.
- Startup founders, entrepreneurs, and product managers can learn what matters in growing their product, how to measure, and how to hold their teams accountable.
- Business students, educators, consultants, and investors/ venture capital (VC) firms can gain a holistic understanding of product growth from this book, which are often critical topics in building and investing in any business.

WHAT THE AUTHORS HOPE YOU GET FROM THIS BOOK

Unlike other books that merely discuss concepts, each chapter in this book is enriched with examples, case studies, and actionable insights that empower you, the reader, to make informed, real-time decisions.

Our book's hands-on approach is intended to not only demystify complex growth metrics and analytics but also to equip professionals—from data scientists to entrepreneurs—with the tactical tools necessary to identify and seize growth opportunities.

We have attempted to foster an engaging learning experience, making our book an indispensable guide for those who strive to drive business success through data-driven strategies. Enjoy this book!

Chapter 1

LEVERAGE GROWTH ANALYTICS TO DRIVE PRODUCT SUCCESS

"A startup is a company designed to grow fast. Being newly founded does not in itself make a company a startup. Nor is it necessary for a startup to work on technology, or take venture funding, or have some sort of 'exit.' The only essential thing is growth. Everything else we associate with startups follows from growth."

—PAUL GRAHAM

As a master sommelier, my friend struggled to sell wine online.

There are a handful of professions where he can claim to be a subject matter expert. After seven years of intense training, he earned the title of "master sommelier." Only 260 people in the world get to this level.

As implied by the word "sommelier," the training emphasizes wine service, making it crucial to understand both the wines and the customers drinking them to recommend the perfect wine.

My friend has this superpower. After some back-and-forth conversation, he is able to provide the best recommendations and delight my senses. Like a good fortune-teller, he gathers insights into my tastes: from my clothes, the way I talk, and my mood. I feel that he knows my preferences better than I do. Of course, on such occasions, he is in his element and can effortlessly sell wine.

But this superpower is lost when he tries to sell online.

And that's the problem most startups struggle with when they grow—*they cannot scale their sense of the customer.*

All successful products with growth potential start with founders with a good sense of their customers. But as the products grow, you will encounter different personas, use cases, demands, scenarios, and much more.

If you succeed in maintaining your customer sense while building products to meet their demands, you keep growing. If you lose that sense, you stop growing.

The only way to maintain your sense of the customer is through data.

This introductory chapter provides an overview of the key concepts and frameworks that are explored throughout the book, setting the foundation for understanding how data drives product growth. From establishing North Star metrics to analyzing user behavior, we'll preview the essential tools and methodologies covered in detail in subsequent chapters. We'll explore how to iterate, optimize, and uncover new opportunities. We'll also discuss what it takes to become a skilled growth analyst. The following chapters dive deeper into specific analytical frameworks.

UNDERSTANDING GROWTH

Without a doubt, all organizations pursue "growth," though its definition can vary widely. For a social media company, it may refer to user growth; for a marketplace, growth may indicate an increase in seller listings; for a charity, it's often about expanding the donor base; and for any for-profit business, it typically means revenue growth. In this book, we will examine the following two key types of growth:

1. **Product-led growth (PLG)** is a business strategy and growth model that leverages the product itself as the primary driver of customer acquisition, retention, conversion, and expansion. In a PLG approach, the product is designed to be intuitive, easy to adopt, and provides immediate value to users, often through a self-service model. This type of growth is ideal for businesses with products that are user-friendly and can cultivate dedicated advocates without requiring extensive assistance. These products typically offer a freemium model that enables users to experience value without a significant up-front investment. Ideally, PLG should possess the potential for viral growth through integrated mechanisms, such as form filling.

2. **Sales-led growth (SLG)** is a business strategy that primarily focuses on increasing revenue through direct sales efforts. The sales team drives the growth of the company and guides potential users through a sales conversion funnel. Sales-led growth places greater emphasis on relationship building, outbound sales efforts, and traditional targeted sales tactics. Sales-led growth is best suited for business-to-business (B2B) companies. SLG isn't entirely separate from PLG—PLG often serves as a strong source of leads for the sales team to engage with. This approach is commonly referred to as **Product-Led Sales (PLS)**.

UNDERSTANDING WHERE YOU ARE IN THE PRODUCT LIFE CYCLE

As you embark on accelerating your growth journey, discussing data becomes nearly inevitable. Indeed, data becomes your closest ally when addressing growth. A fundamental question that many startup founders ask is: At which stage is my product in the product life cycle?

PRODUCT LIFE CYCLE

Numerous effective frameworks exist for evaluating growth at various stages of your product's life cycle. The product life cycle (PLC) is illustrated in Figure 1-1.

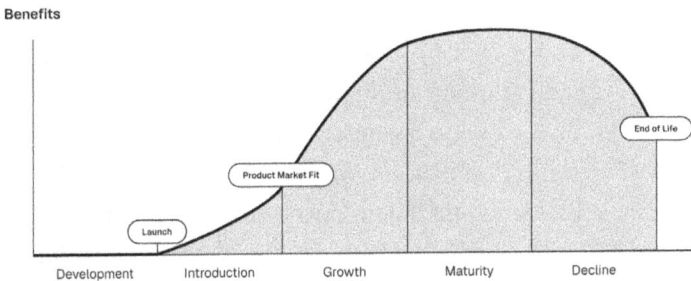

Figure 1-1: Product life cycle

ESTABLISHING A NORTH STAR METRIC

To ensure you are on the right track at different stages, it is important to establish a quantitative measurement to assess your progress compared to the past growth of your product, your competitors, or the industry benchmark. This key growth metric is called the North Star metric. While the North Star metric is thought of as a single metric, it usually includes a few key supporting metrics that influence it. Most recommendations suggest limiting the number of metrics that contribute to a North Star metric to a small number, as using too many metrics can dilute the North Star metric's effectiveness.

The **North Star metric** measures the ultimate success of the product. It motivates the team to prioritize doing the right thing and prevents easily gameable outcomes.

STRATEGIES FOR UNDERSTANDING AND DEFINING YOUR NORTH STAR METRIC

Here are two practical strategies to help you define your North Star metric:

- **Decompose your product mission word by word.** This is a useful starting point when brainstorming metric ideas. If your product's mission is to "enable daily collaboration and connection within your organization," you can break down the mission into "daily," "collaboration," and "connection." Then, determine what metric reflects these elements best on a daily basis. One example is "daily collaborated/engaged teams," where you define "collaborated/engaged" based on the nature of your product, such as sending a message to a coworker or commenting on a coworker's document.
- **Utilize industry-standard metrics.** Social media companies, particularly during their growth or maturity stage, commonly use Monthly Active Users (MAU) as a key metric. MAU provides an estimate of product users and serves as a proxy for ad impressions, which is crucial for companies relying on ad revenue as their primary source of income.

UNDERSTANDING YOUR NORTH STAR METRIC
WITHIN THE GROWTH ACCOUNTING FRAMEWORK

Once you understand what the North Star metric is, you can create and optimize strategies to make it grow. One well-regarded approach to understand and define your North Star metric is the growth accounting framework, which provides a structured way to identify the specific areas that require attention and focus to achieve desired growth.

Growth accounting is an analytical framework for product teams to understand the composition of their North Star metric and how those components drive the North Star metric. Each of the components that drive the growth is a state that is assigned to each unit of the North Star metric on a given day.

For a North Star metric like MAU, growth could be the result of acquiring more new users or more dormant users becoming active again, or fewer users stopping use of the product. For example, imagine a short-form video sharing app had 100 MAU yesterday, and today it reaches 110 MAU, reflecting a growth of 10 users. This increase could result from acquiring 15 new users, reactivating 5 dormant users, and losing 10 users who stopped using the app today.

Decomposing the North Star metric into states that drive its growth can inform growth strategy. From the previous example, let us assign the following states to the users:

- **New users**—Fifteen users who were acquired today.
- **Resurrected users**—Five dormant users who became active today

- **Churned users**—Ten users who stopped using the app today

We can derive a few key insights based on this:

- Reducing churn by 20 percent could have resulted in a 20 percent increase in growth from ten to twelve users. Based on this insight, perform a churn analysis and create a targeted plan to reduce churn by 20 percent.
- If the app retention is stable and new users from certain campaigns or acquisition channels are retentive, then acquire similar users to drive growth.

Growth accounting provides actionable insights for driving product growth. Growth teams can structure themselves based on goals set for the different states of growth accounting. For example, if the app sets a goal of a North Star metric like MAU having a growth rate of 20 percent, based on the decomposition of states, we can derive the goal value for reducing churn. This would translate into a new work stream of growth engineers, product managers (PMs), and data scientists who would build features and systems to achieve those goals for the churn metric.

INCORPORATING GROWTH ANALYTICS INTO YOUR BUSINESS DEVELOPMENT JOURNEY

Once you determine the focus area, you can either rely on intuition or use data and user research to generate hypotheses for the best marketing, product, or sales strategy to grow your business. However, as your business expands, the intuition that guided you with early users may no longer apply to new users. In such cases, it is important to gain a deep understanding of your user mix-shift and identify high-quality users to acquire more of them (see Chapter 3). For existing users, explore ways to keep them engaged (see Chapter 5). While data can provide hypotheses, it is crucial to validate these hypotheses using techniques like experimentation and causal inference analysis (see Experimentation, Chapter 10). All of these techniques are part of the growth analytics suite, which is a collection of tools and techniques designed to help businesses analyze and understand their growth patterns, customer behavior, and market trends.

In this book, the definition of growth analytics is not confined by any company type or organizational structure. This definition applies to growth analytics professionals, as well as anyone interested in analyzing data and generating insights for their business.

> **Reader's cue:** 💡 icons flag "Insight Nuggets"—stand-alone takeaways you can digest in a glance or quote to your team.

> 💡 **Growth analytics** involves using data analysis to directly guide product, marketing, finance, and sales decisions that impact your company's North Star growth metrics, such as increasing user numbers or revenue after the product's initial launch stage.

The "direct" connection to the company's growth North Star metrics sets growth analytics apart from other forms of analytics. For example, while a product analyst may analyze user engagement, their focus is on identifying the key drivers within a particular product area. Their goal might be to uncover issues in the sidebar of a product interface, enabling them to suggest targeted improvements to the product team.

We recommend that founders do not prioritize growth analytics before their product has established its target audience and use case in the market. Initially, the goal should be to identify a very small handful of users who find significant value in your product by conducting in-depth user interviews. This approach enables you to tailor your product to this segment before scaling too quickly and losing focus. Simply put, do not focus on growth before achieving product market fit (PMF). We'll explain more about PMF in Chapter 2.

THE QUALITIES THAT DEFINE GOOD GROWTH ANALYTICS

Whether you are a data science or analytics professional, a founder with a high level of data literacy, or a data-driven founder who is looking to expand your team by hiring more growth analytics experts, it is important for you to have a clear understanding of the key qualities that define good growth analytics.

You may be familiar with growth hacking, a marketing discipline that applies different digital techniques to grow the user base of a product. The practitioners of this discipline are called growth hackers and they are usually part of the growth marketing organization within a company. Growth analytics is typically practiced by data scientists and data analysts at companies to bring an analytical approach to drive sustainable growth.

When searching online for jobs related to growth data scientists or analysts, you often find that requirements include an understanding and experience with experimentation, statistical analysis, and trend investigation. It is important to note that these are just techniques; the fundamental goal of growth analytics is to drive growth. We believe that several key qualities are also essential for becoming an outstanding expert:

- **Scrappiness**—With regard to growth analytics, the term "scrappiness" means trying to accomplish things within constraints, which is particularly important for early stage to midstage startups. Being scrappy in growth analytics means being able to iterate quickly on insights, sharing any early signals that the data reveals, and adjusting analysis as necessary. When the ideal data is not available, scrappiness is about getting creative to obtain proxy data or to advocate building the right data stack to acquire the necessary data.
- **Ability to identify the correct analyses for addressing business questions**—This skill is often developed with experience or effective knowledge acquisition. Many excellent tutorials are available online and in books (including this one!). The key for success is determining the appropriate analyses and techniques to use.

ANALYZING AND ADDRESSING COMMON BUSINESS QUESTIONS WITH A GROWTH ANALYTICS MINDSET

This section provides examples of common business questions and demonstrates how we analyze them for answers. Throughout this book, we delve deeper into each example, and in the final chapter, we offer a reference card to quickly access the techniques required for each analysis.

EXAMPLE 1: HOW CAN WE IMPROVE THE ONBOARDING EXPERIENCE?

Problem context: New users encounter onboarding flows, including registration and first-time use of core features. Understanding how these flows work is essential to enabling users to immediately find value in the product.

Solution: Perform funnel analysis on the different types of user flows. Represent and analyze these flows. Use funnel analysis to measure and identify friction points, and directly highlight investment opportunities that can accelerate product growth.

EXAMPLE 2: IS MY PRODUCT CAPABLE OF ACHIEVING SUSTAINABLE GROWTH?

Problem context: To be successful, products should aim for consistent growth over time while balancing acquisition efforts with the pursuit of sustainable growth. Aggressive acquisition strategies often conceal underlying issues with customer retention. Spending heavily on marketing to attract users who try the product once but do not retain it is a waste of resources and should be avoided.

Solution: Consistently monitor product retention and the growth accounting of your North Star metric to ensure that new user acquisition does not mask churn.

EXAMPLE 3: WHAT ARE THE GROWTH DRIVERS FOR MY PRODUCT?

Problem context: Retaining new users is crucial for sustainable product growth. Understanding the behaviors and features that drive user retention, such as watching relevant and curated videos in a video-first social app like TikTok, is strategically advantageous. These insights help the product team to prioritize and invest in improving the recommendation and discovery engines. These key insights should be discussed when roadmapping a product in the growth phase.

Solution: Analyze behavioral retention to understand:

- The behaviors (actions or events) of users that correlate with short-term and long-term retention.
- The attributes (such as country or age group) of users that correlate with short-term and long-term retention.

Based on these correlations, form hypotheses and run experiments to establish causality.

EXAMPLE 4: WHO ARE THE POWER USERS OF MY PRODUCT?

Problem context: Power users are crucial for maintaining the product's momentum. For example, in a video sharing app, the availability of more videos leads to increased user engagement. As engagement rises, video production also increases. This flywheel of video production, consumption, and engagement keeps the ecosystem thriving and fuels growth. Power users are responsible for keeping these flywheels alive. By understanding and expanding the power user base, the product can achieve sustainable growth.

Solution: Perform a power user analysis.

- Begin a power user analysis by defining who the power users are for your product. One straightforward approach is to examine the number of days users are active on the product. This frequency of use is quantified by a metric called Lness. For example, L28 represents the number of days a user was active in the last twenty-eight days. Users with an L28 value greater than twenty-five can be considered power users. Understanding the journey and behavior of power users is an important asset in developing effective strategies that generate excitement about the product among current users.

EXAMPLE 5: DO WE HAVE A CHURN PROBLEM?

Business context: In your growth accounting dashboard, you see that churn rate has increased by 10 percent month-over-month.

Solution: Perform a failure analysis.

Products often have failure points that can confuse users or cause unexpected behavior. These issues often lead to user churn. For example, during a user journey, such as uploading a video, if users do not receive acknowledgment of the progress or status of the upload, it can leave them confused and frustrated, which often leads them to abandon the user journey.

Track conversion rates for key user journeys to help identify these failure points. Additionally, logging errors and monitoring the trend of errors will provide insights into any product bugs that may be contributing to these failures.

Clear business recommendations: The primary objective of analyzing data or monitoring trends on the dashboard is not only to obtain numerical values but to offer detailed recommendations for future actions that might include suggesting necessary product changes to reduce user churn, identifying key stakeholders for the implementation process, and validating your hypothesis for certain business trajectory changes.

TAKEAWAY

1. Startup = growth. Your startup would likely not succeed without a growth engine. This engine can be powered by sales or by the product itself. In this book, we focus on product-led growth by applying a data-informed strategy to drive growth.

2. Every product goes through different life stages from ideation to building a minimum viable product to achieving product market fit to growth and finally hitting a maturity stage. To ensure you are on the right track at different stages, it is important to establish a quantitative measurement to assess your progress compared to the past growth of your product.

3. A North Star metric measures the ultimate success of the product. It motivates the team to prioritize doing the right thing and prevents easily gameable outcomes. Common North Star metrics for growth are Monthly or Weekly Active Users.

4. Growth accounting is an analytical framework for product teams to understand the composition of their North Star metric and how those components drive the North Star metric.

5. Growth analytics is the use of data to help make smart decisions in product, marketing, finance, and sales that drive a company's key growth goals—like gaining more users or increasing revenue.

EXERCISE

Let's say you are building a habit-tracking app called DailySpark, which helps users build and stick to daily habits like journaling, exercising, or drinking water. The app sends reminders, tracks streaks, and offers insights on habit consistency.

QUESTIONS

Question 1: What should be the North Star metric for DailySpark?

Question 2: What would be two hypothetical growth drivers for DailySpark?

Question 3: How would you identify if DailySpark has a churn problem, and what would you do about it?

ANSWERS

Question 1: What should be the North Star metric for DailySpark?

Answer:

The North Star metric should reflect the core value that users get from the app—helping them stick to habits daily. A good candidate is:

Daily active habit completions—the number of users who complete at least one tracked habit per day.

Question 2: What would be two hypothetical growth drivers for DailySpark?

Answer:

- **Improving onboarding completion rate:** Many users drop off before setting up their first habit. By analyzing onboarding funnel data, the team might discover that users are overwhelmed by too many habit options. Simplifying the onboarding flow and preselecting common habits could increase activation and lead to more users entering the "active" state.
- **Increasing habit streak engagement among returning users:** Behavioral retention analysis may show that users who maintain a three-day streak are far more likely to become long-term users. The product team could run experiments with visual progress tracking or personalized nudges after day two to encourage streak continuation, reducing churn.
- **Encouraging user-generated content and sharing:** A power user analysis might reveal that users who create and share custom habit templates or progress snapshots are not only more engaged but also tend to attract new users. Adding features that make it easy to share streaks on social media or invite friends to join could drive *viral acquisition,* creating a growth loop where engaged users help bring in others.

Question 3: How would you identify if DailySpark has a churn problem, and what would you do about it?

Answer:

To identify churn, you would monitor the *growth accounting breakdown* of your North Star metric (*daily active habit completions*). For example, if your dashboard shows a slowdown in growth despite steady acquisition, it may be due to increased churn.

Here's how to approach it:

- **Check the churn rate:** From your growth accounting dashboard, check if the churn rate has been increasing over time.
- **Perform a failure analysis:**
  - Look for friction points in core user journeys. For instance, users might be dropping off because habit reminders are not delivered on time, or progress is not clearly displayed.
  - Examine feature logs and conversion funnels. For example, is there a sharp drop between users opening the app and completing a habit?

Chapter 2

IDENTIFY EARLY SIGNALS OF PRODUCT VALUE AND SUCCESS

BUILDING A PRODUCT THAT USERS LOVE

Every successful product starts with the fundamental question: Does my product provide real value to users? This is where product market fit (PMF) plays such a critical role in the product development process. View PMF as a compass that directs your product development. According to Meta's analytics blog, PMF is defined as "the value that a given product provides in addressing a specific market segment's need."[1]

---

1   Analytics at Meta, "Analytics and Product-Market Fit," *Medium*, September 7, 2022, https://medium.com/@AnalyticsAtMeta/analytics-and-product-market-fit-11efaea403cd.

Begin this evaluation after the initial prototype phase, when a functional product is ready for customer use.

> 💡 Despite starting with brilliant ideas, many products fail during the PMF stage because they are built on the founders' assumptions rather than actual customer needs.

Understanding PMF involves examining it through three distinct lenses:

1. **The Target Audience Lens.** PMF is segment-specific. Your product does not need to appeal to everyone, but it should excel at meeting your target audience's needs.
2. **The Time Lens.** PMF is not static; it evolves as your product, market, and user needs change. Continuously monitor these changes to maintain alignment.
3. **The Value Lens.** This asserts that, rather than being a simple yes or no question, PMF exists on a spectrum. The key is whether your product delivers enough value to justify scaling.

The following four real-world examples demonstrate why evaluating PMF is so crucial:

- Establishing PMF is essential for growth.
  - Example: BranchOut, a Facebook application launched in 2010, aimed to facilitate job searching, professional networking, and employee recruitment. The app experienced rapid user growth before achieving PMF. Despite raising $49 million, BranchOut's user base declined significantly, prompting the company to pivot.

- PMF helps you predict market success early.
  - Example: An artificial intelligence (AI) chatbot has achieved 50 percent week-over-week growth since its launch, with 80 percent of users renewing their subscriptions.
- PMF validates your competitive edge.
  - Example: A recent survey revealed that 40 percent of new users transitioned from competing AI platforms.
- PMF uncovers unexpected opportunities.
  - Example: While engagement for the AI chatbot in the tech sector fell short of expectations, the engagement for the sports sector is surprisingly good.

THE KEY METRIC FOR PRODUCT MARKET FIT—RETENTION

As you glance at your smartphone, you likely have dozens of installed apps. However, only a handful are part of your daily routine. These apps have proven their value, consistently delivering benefits that earn them a place on your home screen. This illustrates why retention is such a powerful metric for assessing product success.

When evaluating PMF, various indicators come into play, but retention stands out as one of the most critical measures. The concept is straightforward: if users find value in your product, they will keep coming back. Retention is especially useful because it provides meaningful insights even with a small user base. Furthermore, two key properties of retention enhance its significance:

1. Retention offers valuable insights during PMF analysis,

particularly when the user base is small, and feedback is critical.

2. Retention directly correlates with growth potential: successful products increase usage and revenue, fueling further growth.

> In summary, **retention** is the measurement of how many users continue to engage with your product over time, indicating sustained value delivery.

CORE COMPONENTS OF RETENTION ANALYSIS

Measure retention through these four key components:

1. **Active usage definition:** Begin by defining what "active" means for your product. For an AI chatbot, this may involve simply starting one conversation.
2. **Usage frequency parameters:** Next, determine how often users should engage with your product. This frequency varies by product type—messaging apps typically aim for daily use, while travel booking platforms may target monthly engagement.
3. **Time period segmentation:** Analyze user behavior across different time windows: short-term (seven days), mid-term (thirty to sixty days), and long-term (more than 180 days).
4. **Cohort analysis framework:** Finally, group users based on when they first started using the product to track the evolution of retention trends.

Use this formula to calculate retention:

$$\text{Retention rate @ day Y = Retained user}$$
$$\text{volume @ day Y} \div \text{Cohort volume}$$

Where:

- **Retention rate @ day Y** represents the retention percentage after Y days from the first active date.
- **Retained user volume @ day Y** denotes the number of users who are still active after Y days.
- **Cohort volume** indicates the initial group size.

Here's a real-world example to illustrate retention calculation. Imagine launching a new app on New Year's Day 2022, attracting one hundred enthusiastic users on day one. Fast forward to January 8: your analytics dashboard shows that twenty of those initial users are still actively using your app on that day.

Now calculate the Daily Active Users (DAU) retention rate for day seven: it would be 20 percent (twenty active users divided by one hundred initial users). This simple calculation reveals crucial insights into how well your app retains users after their first week.

VISUALIZING RETENTION PATTERNS

When users first discover your product, some will stay while others will drift away. This journey of user engagement over time creates a *retention curve*. For business-to-consumer (B2C) products, this curve often presents an interesting narrative—it starts with a sharp decline as casual users leave. Then something significant happens: the curve begins to flatten out, forming a "J" shape, as you identify true believers—users who genuinely find value in your offering.

> 💡 Keep in mind that these curves are not one-size-fits-all—retention curves can look quite different depending on your product type and who you are serving.

Plotting the percentage of retained users against time reveals more than just numbers; it provides insight into how people use your product. Whether analyzing days, weeks, or months, this visual representation helps determine if you are building something that will endure.

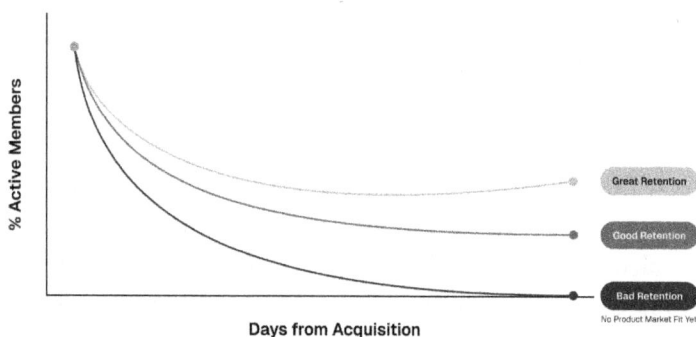

Figure 2-1: Retention curve patterns

Next, examine three different retention curve patterns shown in Figure 2-1 and what they tell us about product success:

The Ideal Scenario—The Smile

The top line represents the dream scenario for any product team. Users not only stay, but some who left also return. This "smiling" curve is rare and typically appears only in exceptional products that become indispensable tools for users.

The Healthy Reality—The Plateau

The middle line represents a healthy, sustainable product. An initial decline occurs as casual users leave, but a solid core group discovers lasting value and remains engaged. This pattern represents the goal for most successful products.

The Warning Sign—The Decline

If your retention looks like the bottom line—a continuous decline—it's crucial to pause growth initiatives and prioritize fixing the product's core value proposition.

To track these patterns accurately, use cohort tables. These tables allow for analysis of how retention changes among groups of users who began using the product at the same time. While cohort analysis requires a substantial user base to yield meaningful insights, remember that these comparisons reveal trends rather than absolute statistical certainty.

Retention rates by weeks after sign-up

Cohort	New Users	1	2	3	4	5	6	7	8	9	10	11	12	13	14	15	16	17
Apr 27, 2014	79	22%	19%	13%	19%	16%	23%	19%	20%	11%	14%	16%	10%	10%	10%	8.9%	6.3%	6.3%
May 04, 2014	168	23%	21%	21%	24%	24%	29%	24%	18%	22%	14%	14%	12%	13%	9.5%	9.5%	6.5%	
May 11, 2014	188	19%	19%	13%	21%	19%	20%	24%	21%	16%	14%	13%	10%	9.0%	9.0%	7.4%		
May 18, 2014	191	23%	21%	22%	22%	26%	27%	29%	26%	21%	21%	17%	15%	10%	5.8%			
May 25, 2014	191	21%	16%	20%	24%	27%	23%	20%	19%	15%	15%	12%	12%	5.8%				
Jun 01, 2014	184	24%	24%	24%	24%	21%	21%	18%	20%	16%	15%	18%	6.5%					
Jun 08, 2014	182	19%	16%	25%	19%	23%	28%	22%	18%	13%	9.9%	4.9%						
Jun 15, 2014	209	24%	20%	24%	22%	22%	17%	18%	15%	13%	7.2%							
Jun 22, 2014	217	22%	19%	19%	20%	20%	17%	19%	15%	12%								
Jun 29, 2014	221	16%	18%	24%	24%	23%	19%	20%	7.7%									
Jul 06, 2014	203	24%	23%	18%	16%	24%	22%	16%										
Jul 13, 2014	188	24%	18%	20%	18%	21%	9.6%											
Jul 20, 2014	228	19%	14%	14%	14%	7.5%												
Jul 27, 2014	204	14%	12%	15%	11%													
Aug 03, 2014	230	22%	17%	11%														
Aug 10, 2014	245	16%	8.2%															
Aug 17, 2014	252	12%																
Aug 24, 2014	251																	

Figure 2-2: Cohort table

Reading a Cohort Table

To better understand how to read a cohort table, first think of a cohort as a way to view your data from three different angles, each revealing its own story about user behavior.

Begin with the horizontal axis, which tracks a single group of users over time. For example, consider the May 18 cohort. If this group demonstrates unusually high engagement after five weeks, it signals that a recent change—perhaps a new feature or improvement—resonated well with these users.

Retention rates by weeks after sign-up

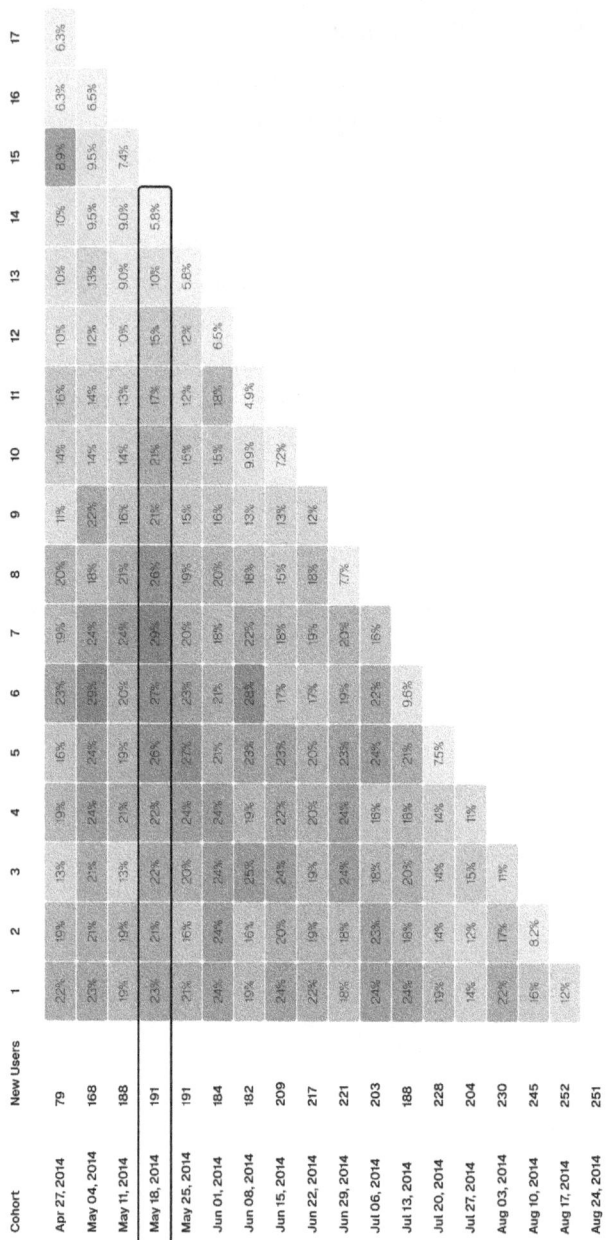

Cohort	New Users	1	2	3	4	5	6	7	8	9	10	11	12	13	14	15	16	17
Apr 27, 2014	79	22%	19%	13%	19%	16%	23%	19%	20%	11%	14%	16%	10%	10%	10%	8.9%	6.3%	6.3%
May 04, 2014	168	23%	21%	21%	24%	24%	23%	24%	18%	22%	14%	14%	12%	13%	9.5%	9.5%	6.5%	
May 11, 2014	188	19%	19%	13%	21%	19%	20%	24%	21%	16%	14%	13%	10%	9.0%	9.0%	7.4%		
May 18, 2014	191	23%	21%	22%	22%	26%	27%	29%	26%	21%	21%	17%	15%	10%	5.8%			
May 25, 2014	191	21%	16%	20%	24%	27%	23%	20%	19%	15%	15%	12%	12%	5.8%				
Jun 01, 2014	184	24%	24%	24%	24%	21%	21%	18%	20%	16%	15%	18%	6.5%					
Jun 08, 2014	182	19%	16%	25%	19%	23%	28%	22%	18%	13%	9.9%	4.9%						
Jun 15, 2014	209	24%	20%	24%	22%	23%	17%	18%	15%	13%	7.2%							
Jun 22, 2014	217	22%	19%	19%	20%	20%	17%	19%	18%	12%								
Jun 29, 2014	221	18%	18%	24%	24%	23%	19%	20%	7.7%									
Jul 06, 2014	203	24%	23%	20%	16%	24%	22%	16%										
Jul 13, 2014	188	24%	16%	18%	18%	21%	9.6%											
Jul 20, 2014	228	19%	14%	14%	14%	7.5%												
Jul 27, 2014	204	14%	12%	15%	11%													
Aug 03, 2014	230	22%	17%	11%														
Aug 10, 2014	245	16%	8.2%															
Aug 17, 2014	252	12%																
Aug 24, 2014	251																	

Figure 2-3: Retention rates by weeks after sign-ups

The vertical axis reveals how the product evolves over time. Each row represents a different group of users who began using the product in various weeks. Ideally, as product improvements occur, newer groups of users should demonstrate longer retention than older groups.

Examine the data. After week three, a clear pattern emerges: retention improves with each new group of users, indicating that product enhancements are effective. However, user retention dropped unexpectedly for users who joined after July 6, signaling a potential issue that warrants investigation. Was it due to a feature change or a bug? Understanding this decline can help regain momentum.

Retention rates by weeks after sign-up

Cohort	New Users	1	2	3	4	5	6	7	8	9	10	11	12	13	14	15	16	17
Apr 27, 2014	79	22%	19%	13%	19%	16%	23%	19%	20%	11%	14%	16%	10%	10%	10%	8.9%	6.3%	6.3%
May 04, 2014	168	25%	21%	21%	24%	24%	29%	24%	18%	22%	14%	14%	12%	13%	9.5%	9.5%	6.5%	
May 11, 2014	188	19%	19%	13%	21%	19%	20%	24%	21%	16%	14%	13%	10%	9.0%	9.0%	7.4%		
May 18, 2014	191	23%	21%	22%	22%	26%	27%	29%	20%	21%	21%	17%	15%	10%	5.8%			
May 25, 2014	191	21%	16%	20%	24%	27%	23%	20%	19%	16%	15%	12%	12%	5.8%				
Jun 01, 2014	184	24%	24%	24%	24%	21%	21%	18%	20%	16%	15%	18%	6.5%					
Jun 08, 2014	182	19%	16%	25%	19%	23%	28%	22%	18%	13%	9.9%	4.9%						
Jun 15, 2014	209	24%	20%	24%	22%	23%	17%	18%	15%	13%	7.2%							
Jun 22, 2014	217	22%	19%	19%	20%	20%	17%	19%	16%	12%								
Jun 29, 2014	221	18%	18%	24%	24%	23%	19%	20%	7.7%									
Jul 06, 2014	203	24%	23%	18%	16%	24%	22%	16%										
Jul 13, 2014	188	24%	18%	20%	18%	21%	9.6%											
Jul 20, 2014	228	19%	14%	14%	14%	7.5%												
Jul 27, 2014	204	14%	12%	15%	11%													
Aug 03, 2014	230	22%	17%	11%														
Aug 10, 2014	245	16%	8.2%															
Aug 17, 2014	252	12%																
Aug 24, 2014	251																	

Figure 2-4: Observing the retention rates of different cohorts over a period of time

The diagonal axis uncovers insights about events on specific calendar dates. For example, on August 17, an unusual trend emerged. Nearly every group of users, regardless of their start date, experienced a sudden decline in engagement. Such a pattern typically indicates a specific event that impacted all users simultaneously. Consider the possibility of a technical issue in the production environment or an external factor in a key market that caused decreased user activity. This diagonal view prompts investigation into these questions, guiding improvements and response.

Retention rates by weeks after sign-up

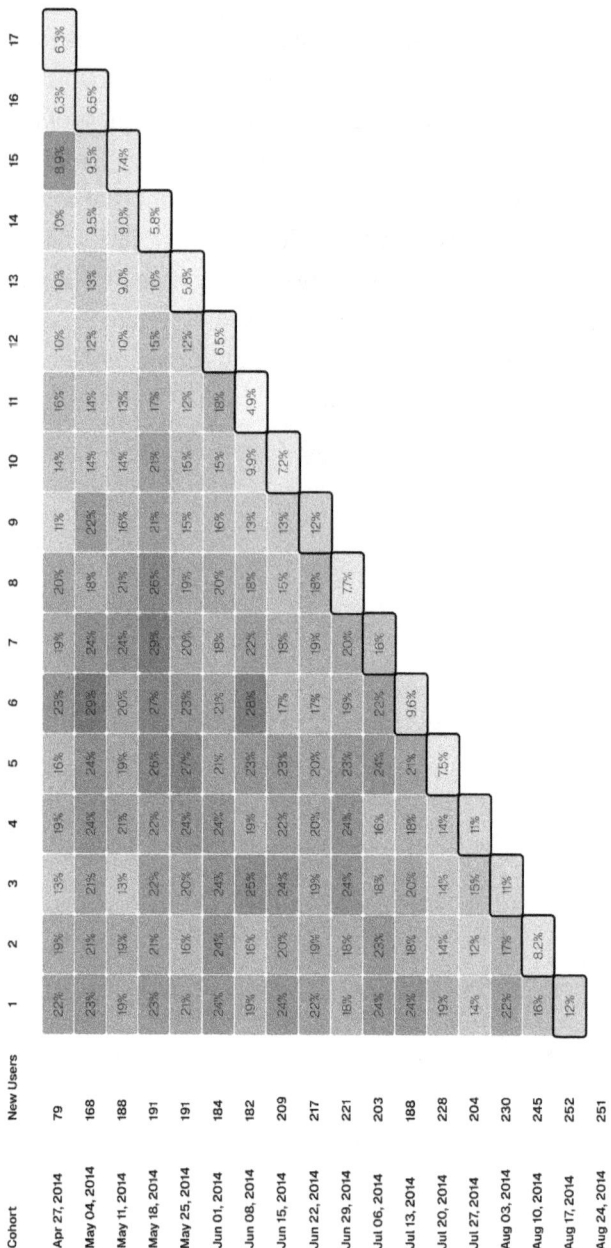

Cohort	New Users	1	2	3	4	5	6	7	8	9	10	11	12	13	14	15	16	17
Apr 27, 2014	79	22%	19%	13%	19%	16%	23%	19%	20%	11%	14%	16%	10%	10%	10%	8.9%	6.3%	6.3%
May 04, 2014	168	23%	21%	21%	24%	24%	29%	24%	18%	22%	14%	14%	12%	13%	9.5%	9.5%	6.5%	
May 11, 2014	188	19%	19%	13%	21%	19%	20%	24%	21%	16%	14%	13%	10%	9.0%	9.0%	7.4%		
May 18, 2014	191	23%	21%	22%	22%	26%	27%	29%	26%	21%	21%	17%	15%	10%	5.8%			
May 25, 2014	191	21%	16%	20%	24%	27%	23%	20%	19%	15%	15%	12%	12%	5.8%				
Jun 01, 2014	184	24%	24%	24%	24%	21%	21%	18%	20%	16%	15%	18%	6.5%					
Jun 08, 2014	182	19%	16%	25%	19%	23%	28%	22%	18%	13%	9.9%	4.9%						
Jun 15, 2014	209	24%	20%	24%	22%	23%	17%	18%	15%	13%	7.2%							
Jun 22, 2014	217	22%	19%	19%	20%	20%	17%	19%	18%	12%								
Jun 29, 2014	221	18%	18%	24%	24%	23%	19%	20%	7.7%									
Jul 06, 2014	203	24%	23%	18%	16%	24%	23%	16%										
Jul 13, 2014	188	24%	18%	20%	18%	21%	9.6%											
Jul 20, 2014	228	19%	14%	14%	14%	7.5%												
Jul 27, 2014	204	14%	12%	15%	11%													
Aug 03, 2014	230	22%	17%	11%														
Aug 10, 2014	245	16%	8.2%															
Aug 17, 2014	252	12%																
Aug 24, 2014	251																	

Figure 2-5: Changes in retention across different cohorts on a specific calendar date

IS MY RETENTION GOOD ENOUGH?

After launching a product, you might ask, "Are we on the right track?" This is where retention becomes essential—it's your product's report card, telling you whether users find genuine value in what you've created.

Similar to a doctor assessing multiple vital signs during a health checkup, evaluate several indicators to understand if your retention is truly "good enough." Follow this diagnostic approach:

1. **Conduct a self-check:** Review your own progress over time. Are newer user groups remaining longer than earlier ones? This trend indicates whether learning and improving are taking place.

2. **Get a second opinion:** Review similar products in your space. For example, if you are building an AI chatbot, compare your retention rates to established customer service messaging apps. This provides you with valuable context about what "good" looks like in your market.

Short-term retention (WAU@D14)

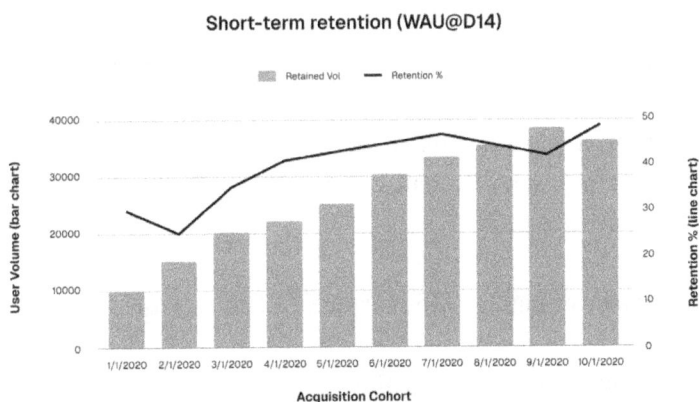

Figure 2-6: Example of short-term retention by acquisition cohort. WAU is Weekly Active User, which counts how many users were active on your product for at least once per week.

AVOID THESE COMMON RETENTION STRATEGY PITFALLS

Here are lessons from four product managers who learned valuable lessons about retention metrics the hard way:

- Sarah eagerly adopted the same retention metrics that Netflix had publicized, thinking, *If it works for them, it'll work for us!* She quickly discovered that her meditation app had different usage patterns than a social network. While users who meditated once a week could be highly engaged, daily media use was the norm.
- Mike proudly shared that his product's 20 percent short-term retention rate surpassed a competitor's 15 percent rate. However, he overlooked a key detail: his team defined retention based on logins, while the competitor tracked actual feature usage.
- Alex believed that she could relax after achieving product market fit. *With great retention, we can focus on growth now!* she thought. Six months later, she was shocked to find retention had plummeted as the user base transitioned from early tech adopters to mainstream users.
- Jamie attempted to use retention metrics for quick decisions on new features and soon learned the hard way that retention is a lagging indicator. It took weeks to observe the true impact of changes, making it unsuitable for rapid experimentation.

These stories highlight four critical pitfalls to avoid:

1. **Avoid copying metrics blindly from other products:** Your product's unique characteristics require a tailored retention framework.

2. **Exercise caution with retention comparisons:** Different measurement methods can lead to misleading conclusions.
3. **Continue monitoring retention:** Even after achieving PMF, both your user base and product will evolve.
4. **Recognize retention's delayed nature:** Quick decisions rely on different metrics; retention reveals a longer-term narrative.

CASE STUDY

Consider an exciting mobile game currently in development. Imagine fruits and vegetables falling from the sky as players swipe their screens to slice them, earning points for each successful cut. This concept is simple, engaging, and potentially addictive. But how can the team ensure they are building something users truly want?

To address this question, retention becomes a focal point, serving as one of the strongest indicators of PMF. Before diving into the data, it is essential to establish a clear measurement framework.

SETTING THE MEASUREMENT FRAMEWORK

Three key metrics define success:

1. **Defining an "active" user:** A user qualifies as active if they play for at least ten seconds. This threshold helps differentiate genuine players and accidental opens.
2. **Determine engagement frequency:** Given that each level only takes a few minutes, the goal is to achieve daily engagement, aligning with the casual gaming pattern being targeted.

3. **Identifying success measurement timelines:** Track reten-
   tion across three important time frames:
   A. **Seven-day mark:** Do players return after their first
      week?
   B. **Sixty-day milestone:** Has the game become part of
      their regular gaming routine?
   C. **One hundred eighty-day horizon:** Is the game provid-
      ing lasting entertainment value?

With these metrics in place, the team is ready to track effectiveness of the game in keeping players engaged and coming
back for more.

Retention Curve

Retention curve for mobile gaming app

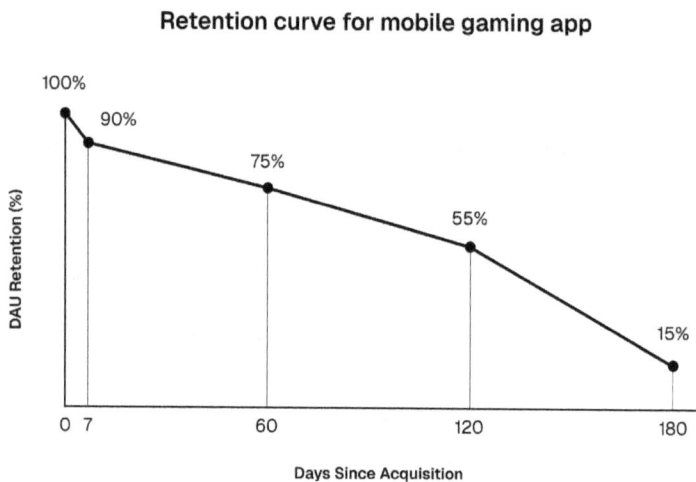

Figure 2-7: Hypothetical retention curve for a mobile gaming app

The retention data for the mobile game shows three distinct
phases:

1. **Strong initial engagement:** Users actively explore the game during the first few weeks.
2. **Mid-term decline:** User engagement noticeably declines after the initial period.
3. **Long-term drop-off:** A significant decrease in active users occurs over an extended time frame. The analysis indicates that users often stop playing upon reaching a specific level, which is the terminal level of the game.

Retention metric trend across cohorts

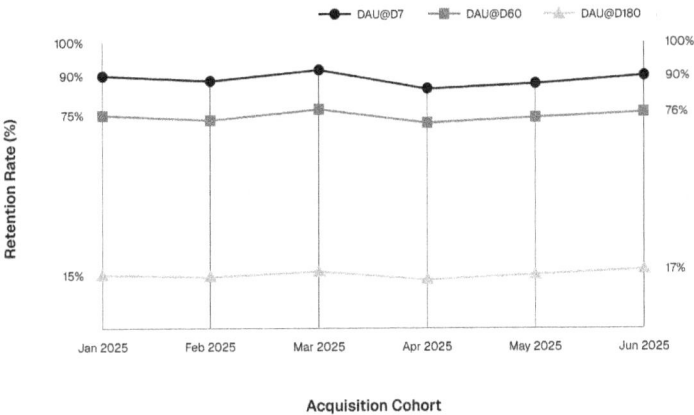

Figure 2-8: Retention metric trend across cohort

Analysis of the time series across short-term (DAU@7), mid-term (WAU@60) and long-term (MAU@180) retention metrics across cohorts revealed no concerning trends; the lower long-term retention was not exclusive to recent players. Instead, a clear pattern emerged: players consistently stopped playing after reaching the game's final level. This phenomenon is similar to finishing a captivating book—when no new content remains, players naturally move on.

Product Optimization Opportunities

The thirteen to eighteen age group exhibited lower retention rates compared to other age groups. User research indicated that these younger users do not resonate with traditional fruits like apples and watermelons. Instead, they prefer fictional fruits and foods popularized by media and influencers.

DAU@D7 retention by age group

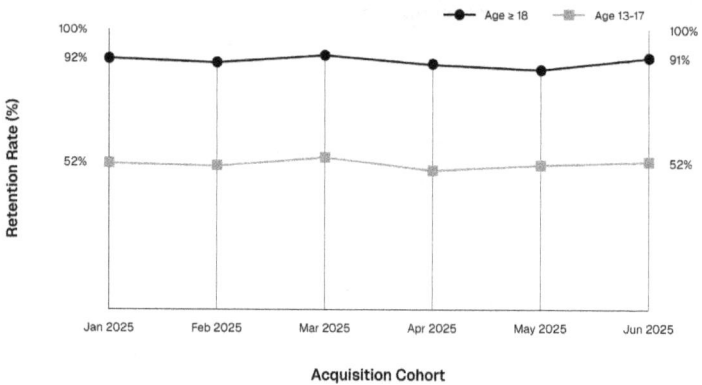

Figure 2-9: Short-term retention by age group across cohorts

During the analysis of retention rates by country, we discovered significantly lower rates appeared in Asia. User research revealed that the fruits featured in the game were unfamiliar to Asian players. By modifying the game to incorporate locally popular fruits for each geography, users were able to connect more deeply to the gameplay, resulting in improved retention and growth.

DAU@D7 retention by geographic region

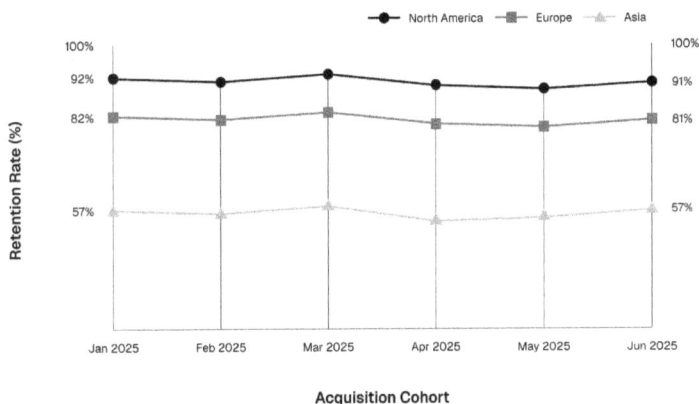

Figure 2-10: Short-term retention across geographic regions

SOLUTION

To address this challenge, the team drew inspiration from storytelling. Just as new chapters rejuvenate a beloved book, exciting themed levels were crafted to keep players engaged. In Asian markets, locally popular fruits were introduced, providing instant recognition for players. To keep content fresh, fruits rotated based on trending topics and seasonal themes. Targeted in-app promotions were designed to entice players to return and experience these culturally tailored additions.

RESULTS

The strategy yielded impressive results. By tracking cohort J curves (those handy graphs that show user engagement over time), it became clear that players returned to embrace these new adventures, revitalizing the game.

Retention curve by cohort (Jan–Mar 2025)

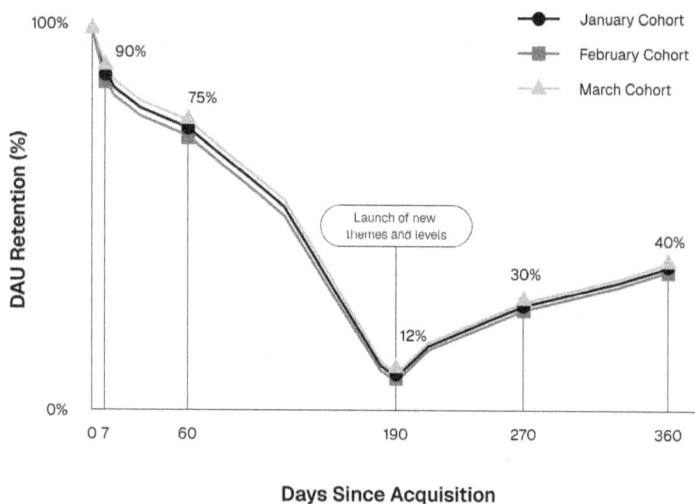

January Cohort
February Cohort
March Cohort

DAU Retention (%)

100%
90%
75%

Launch of new
themes and levels

40%
30%
12%

0%

0 7   60   190   270   360

Days Since Acquisition

Figure 2-11: Retention curves by monthly cohorts after launch of new themes and levels

ADDRESS LAGGING RETENTION
WITH LEADING INDICATORS

Imagine launching a new feature and eagerly awaiting user feedback. The traditional approach involves assessing long-term retention. For example, identifying who's still using your product after 180 days. However, this method has a drawback: waiting that long can mean critical missed opportunities for improvement or strategic pivots.

This is where "activation" becomes crucial. Think of it as an early warning system that helps to predict long-term success. Just as a doctor can anticipate health risks by evaluating vital signs, teams can forecast user retention by analyzing specific early behaviors.

Instead of waiting 180 days to determine whether users remain engaged, focus on defined actions taken in the first two weeks. These early signals can tell us if we're on the right track, facilitating quicker and more informed decisions.

The advantage of this method extends beyond retention; similar early indicators can predict other outcomes. For example, the likelihood of converting a user into a paying customer.

To select the right early signals to track, consider three essential qualities:

- **Predictability:** Like a weather forecast, the signal should accurately predict future behavior.
- **Measurability:** It's essential to quickly identify changes, particularly during experiments.
- **Simplicity:** Ensure that every team member understands what is measured and why.

FINDING THE LEADING INDICATOR
FOR LONG-TERM SUCCESS

Imagine building a video streaming app. You notice that users who watch more than ten minutes of content in their first week are more likely to become long-term users. This is known as a *leading indicator*—an early signal that predicts future success. Meta discovered that users who made ten friends in their first week were more likely to stay. These "aha moments" are essential for understanding your product's success.

To identify these pivotal moments, consider two key components:

1. **The What:** Start by pinpointing the behaviors that may indicate success. For a video app, relevant metrics include watch time, number of videos, or length of viewing sessions.

2. **The When:** Next, determine your measurement window. If you need quick feedback for marketing, examine day one behavior. For deeper engagement insights, utilize a seven-day window.

Once you define these components, create specific metrics to track. For example, use this metric: "users who watch more than ten minutes of video in their first seven days." These become your *candidate indicators*.

However, not all indicators hold equal value. To identify the most effective ones, use the F1 score. This metric balances precision (the proportion of users satisfying your criteria) and recall (the proportion of loyal users meeting your criteria). Think of it as finding the sweet spot between being too strict and too lenient in your predictions.

$$F_1 = 2 \frac{precision \times recall}{precision + recall} = \frac{TP}{TP + \frac{1}{2}(FP + FN)}$$

TP = number of true positives

FP = number of false positives

FN = number of false negatives

Visualizing these concepts enhances understanding of how F1 scores evaluate different metrics and identify the most reliable predictors of user retention.

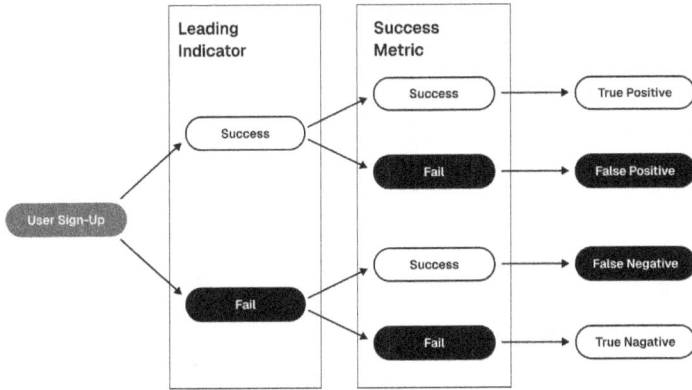

Figure 2-12: Leading Indicator Validation: Prediction vs. Actual Outcomes. Measuring predictability with the F1 score.

After calculating precision and recall, create a plot to assess which metrics excel in different areas of the F1 score.

Each dot on the chart represents a distinct metric being evaluated:

- **The x-axis (Precision):** Indicates prediction accuracy; a higher percentage means that the metric effectively identifies actual long-term users.
- **The y-axis (Recall):** Reflects the proportion of actual long-term users the metric captures; a higher percentage means that the metric recognizes more loyal users.

The dots scattered across the chart demonstrate the trade-off between precision and recall—typically, as precision increases, recall decreases, and vice versa. The ideal metrics appear in the top-right corner and indicate high precision and high recall.

This visualization empowers product teams to evaluate various metrics and find the optimal balance between being too strict (high precision, low recall) and too lenient (low precision, high recall) in their predictions.

Precision vs. recall

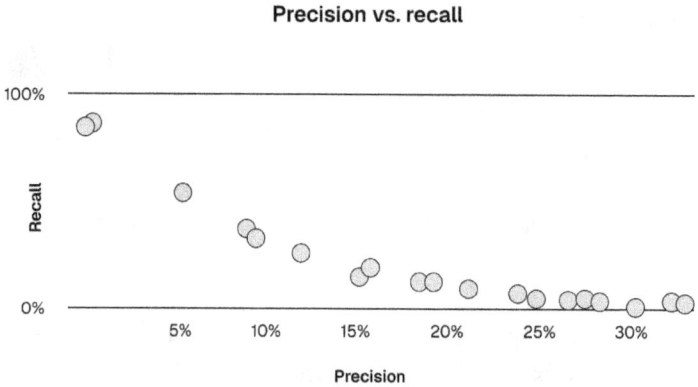

Figure 2-13: Plotting the precision and recall values

Another approach to understanding predictability involves using machine learning (ML) models like decision trees or logistic regression with L1 (a.k.a. LASSO) regularization, to identify candidates that strongly correlate with retention. For example, when using a decision tree, if the first split occurs at "number of videos watched in the first seven days is greater than ten," this metric serves as the best predictor of retention.

Retention drivers for short form video consumption app

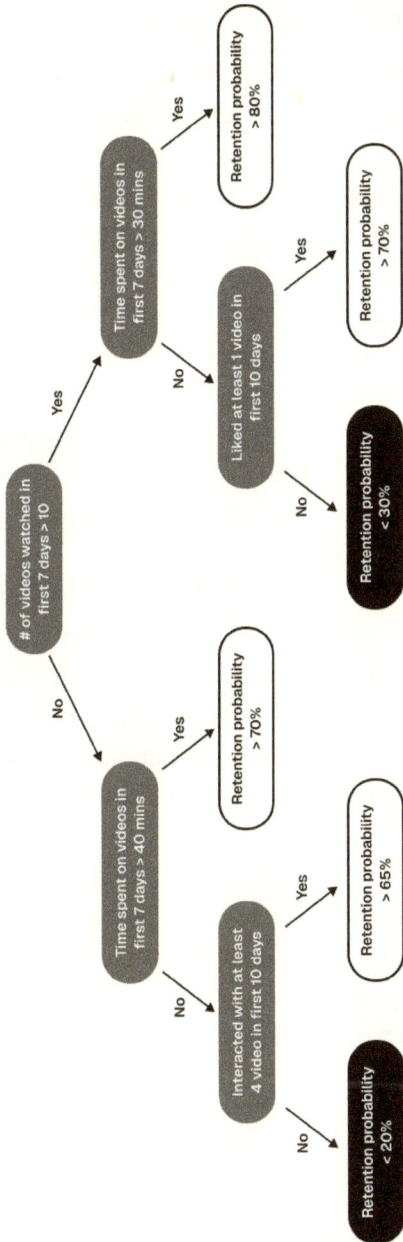

Figure 2-14: Decision tree of deciding early indicators

MEASURABILITY

Measurability involves evaluating how quickly significant metric changes can be statistically detected. To assess a metric's measurability, calculate the time needed to detect a significant percentage change using your user traffic—whether at full or half volume—during experiments. Utilize standard t-test sample size calculations or readily available R and Python packages for determining experimental sample sizes. For example, if a metric requires a month to detect a 20 percent change, consider replacing it, as smaller changes will require even longer experiment durations, which can hinder timely decision-making.

COMBINING PREDICTABILITY AND MEASURABILITY

After calculating both the predictability score and the number of days required to detect significant metric changes, create a plot to visualize these results. This plot helps identify which metrics offer the best combination of predictability and measurability, with each dot representing a metric candidate.

When multiple metrics exhibit similar F_1 scores and measurability, subjective considerations in metrics selection become important. Often, the best leading indicator metric is determined by *simplicity*. For example, if a single-action metric suffices instead of a three-action metric, opt for the simpler option.

CAVEATS

A critical caveat about leading indicator metrics is that their relevance to long-term retention may change over time. This shift can result from changes in the user base or the introduction of new features for new users. Therefore, continuously monitor the predictability and measurability of these metrics and reevaluate their effectiveness at least once a year.

CASE STUDY ON LEADING INDICATOR

Let's examine a real-world example of this methodology. As a data scientist working on a video streaming app, your product manager asks you to create a metric to monitor experiments—specifically, one that strongly correlates with long-term retention.

Building on our earlier discussion around criteria for identifying potential leading indicators, several potential metrics have been generated and analyzed for their precision, recall, and F1 scores (shown in Table 2-1). The data highlights an interesting trade-off between precision and recall.

The metric column displays three types of measurements tracked over a seven-day period:

- **ActiveHour_Day7_LongerThan_X:** Measures whether users are active for more than X hours within their first seven days.
- **NumberOfVideo_Day7_MoreThan_X:** Tracks whether users watch more than X videos within their first seven days.
- **LongestVideoMin_Day7_LongerThan_X:** Measures if users watch any single video longer than X minutes within their first seven days.

Each metric features different thresholds (the X values) to determine which level of engagement best predicts user retention.

METRIC	PRECISION	RECALL	F1 SCORE
ActiveHour_Day7_LongerThan_1	0.60	0.75	0.6666667
ActiveHour_Day7_LongerThan_2	0.70	0.65	0.6740741
ActiveHour_Day7_LongerThan_3	0.90	0.10	0.1800000
NumberOfVideo_Day7_MoreThan_1	0.50	0.85	0.6296296
NumberOfVideo_Day7_MoreThan_2	0.55	0.75	0.6346154
NumberOfVideo_Day7__MoreThan_3	0.65	0.45	0.5318182
LongestVideoMin_Day7__LongerThan_10	0.40	0.55	0.4631579
LongestVideoMin_Day7__LongerThan_20	0.63	0.46	0.5317431
LongestVideoMin_Day7__LongerThan_30	0.70	0.34	0.4576923
LongestVideoMin_Day7__LongerThan_60	0.85	0.25	0.3863636

Table 2-1: Brainstorm candidates metrics

Producing these points on the chart reveals that watch hours exceeding two hours within the first seven days after the user sign up offer the best balance of precision and recall.

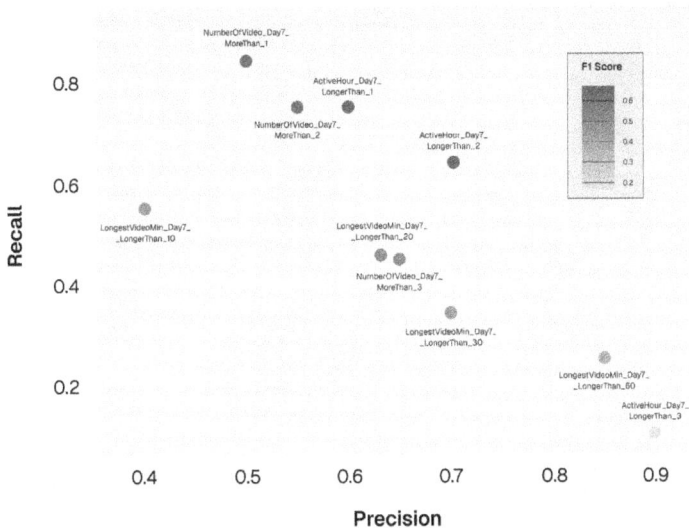

Figure 2-15: Precision and recall for early indicator candidates

To evaluate whether this metric can be detected swiftly enough for experiments, plot the F1 score against power analysis results. The power analysis reveals the sample size required to detect a 10 percent change in the metric. By dividing this sample size by your weekly user traffic, you can calculate the observation time necessary for meaningful changes. In this case, detecting a 10 percent change takes approximately ten days, which aligns well with a standard two-week experiment window. This makes it an excellent candidate for measuring long-term effects of changes on users.

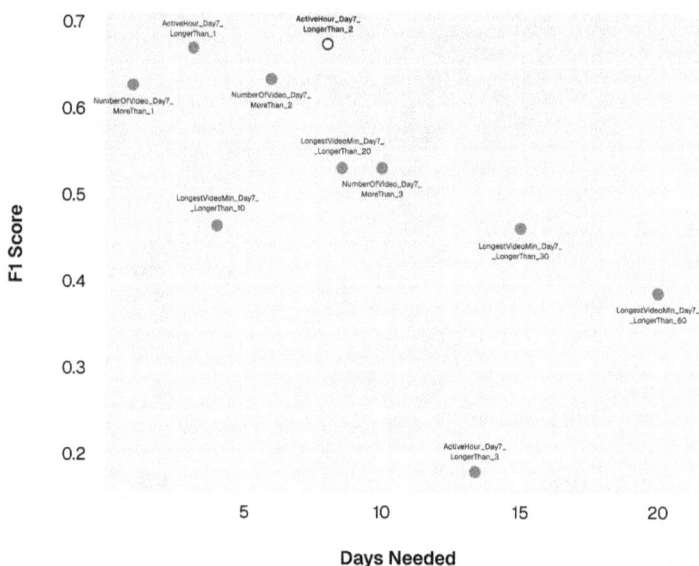

Figure 2-16: Days needed for a meaningful change of the metric in an experiment

TAKEAWAY

Companies like LinkedIn have made retention a central focus. They specifically monitored whether users returned after six months—a significant duration in the fast-paced tech world. The reason is clear: if users continue to engage with LinkedIn after half a year, they're likely finding genuine value in the platform.

What makes retention such a powerful metric? First, its simplicity stands out. Whether discussing with team members or investors, everyone understands the fundamental question: Are users returning or not? Second, retention provides a historical perspective on product performance. By analyzing how different user groups remain engaged over time (referred to as "retention curves"), you can determine whether your product changes are making a meaningful difference.

1. To measure retention effectively, combine these three key ingredients:
   A. A clear definition of what "active" means for your product.
   B. An understanding of how frequently users should naturally use your product.
   C. A specific time period to measure.
2. Retention helps in three crucial ways:
   A. It provides a strong indicator of product market fit, helping you to assess whether you are creating something that people generally want.
   B. It identifies which user groups value your product most, enabling you to discover similar users.
   C. It highlights user behaviors that lead to long-term loyalty, informing you on what to promote.
3. However, retention comes with a caveat—it is like looking in the rearview mirror. Therefore, proactive teams also track early warning signs that can predict retention. Consider these leading indicators as your product's vital signs, enabling you to identify problems before they escalate.

EXERCISE

You are a data scientist at a mobile gaming company. Your game is free to play with in-app purchases. You have the following data for users who installed the game in January 2024:

USER ID	GAMES PLAYED (WEEK 1)	TIME SPENT (WEEK 1)	IN-APP PURCHASES (WEEK 1)	RETAINED AT DAY 30?
1001	25	180 min	$0	Yes
1002	5	30 min	$0	No
1003	15	120 min	$4.99	Yes
1004	30	240 min	$9.99	Yes
1005	3	15 min	$0	No

Table 2-2: User metrics for gaming app

QUESTIONS

Question 1: Calculate the precision and recall for the following potential leading indicators:

- A. Users who play more than ten games in Week 1
- B. Users who spend more than sixty minutes playing in Week 1
- C. Users who make any in-app purchase in Week 1

Question 2: Which metric has the highest F1 score?

Question 3: Based on these results, what would you recommend as the leading indicator for this game?

ANSWERS

Question 1: Calculate the precision and recall for the following potential leading indicators:

A. **Games > 10:** Precision = 3/3 = 1.00 Recall = 3/3 = 1.00
F1 Score = 2 × (1.00 × 1.00) ÷ (1.00 + 1.00) = 1.00

B. **Time > 60 min:** Precision = 3/3 = 1.00 Recall = 3/3 = 1.00 F1 Score = 1.00

C. **Any purchase:** Precision = 2/2 = 1.00 Recall = 2/3 = 0.67 F1 Score = 2 × (1.00 × 0.67) ÷ (1.00 + 0.67) = 0.80

Question 2: Which metric has the highest F1 score?

The metrics "Games > 10" and "Time > 60 min" are tied for the highest F1 score at 1.00.

Question 3: Based on these results, what would you recommend as the leading indicator for this game?

Recommendation: Use "Games > 10" as the leading indicator because:

A. It has best precision and recall in this sample.

B. It's easier to measure than time spent.

C. It's more actionable for the product team to design features around the number of games played.

Chapter 3

BUILD THE FOUNDATION WITH GROWTH ACCOUNTING FRAMEWORK

💡 Every company should track the growth accounting component of their North Star metric.

THE GROWTH ACCOUNTING FRAMEWORK

Growth accounting is like maintaining a detailed health record for your business or product. For example, if you are tracking app usage, growth accounting helps you understand exactly where users originate and where they navigate within the app. It's similar to reviewing your bank statement to monitor money coming in and going out, except here, you are tracking user activity.

Growth accounting helps you in three primary ways:

- **It helps you understand what's really driving your growth:** whether it's new users signing up, existing users staying active, or former users coming back.
- **It alerts you to potential problems early:** whether too many users are leaving (churning) or you are not attracting enough new users.
- **It helps you make better decisions about where to focus your efforts for driving growth:** whether that's improving user retention, acquiring new users, or reengaging lost users.

UNDERSTANDING USER GROWTH: AN INTRODUCTION TO GROWTH ACCOUNTING

Every product has users, and tracking their growth is essential. **User growth accounting** helps understand how users interact with a product over time by doing the following:

- Analyze user engagement history.
- Measure the impact of new user acquisition.
- Track retention and churn rates.

The growth accounting framework provides crucial insights into a company's growth. In this chapter, we'll first explore this framework in detail, and explore other growth accounting methods later in the chapter.

CREATING A GROWTH ACCOUNTING FRAMEWORK
Core Components

A growth accounting framework comprises four essential elements:

1. Unit

This is the fundamental element you track, typically aligned with your North Star metric. For example, in Monthly Active Users (MAU), one unit represents one user.

2. Active Status

Clearly define what makes a unit "active." This should reflect meaningful engagement with your product. For example:

- **Video app:** Watching content for at least ten seconds
- **Chat app:** Successfully sending a message

3. Time Granularity

Choose how often you'll measure user activity (daily, weekly, monthly). This choice should align with your desired user engagement frequency.

4. State Transitions

Monitor how units move between active and inactive status. The five main statuses are:

- **New:** First-time users
- **Retained:** Users active yesterday and today

- **Churned:** Users active yesterday who are inactive today
- **Resurrected:** Users inactive yesterday who became active today (not first-time)
- **Stale:** Users inactive both yesterday and today

Note: These states can be measured at daily, weekly, or monthly intervals.

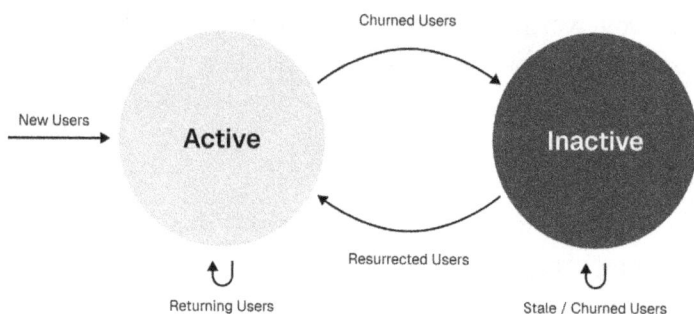

Figure 3-1: Growth accounting states

Fundamental User Growth Accounting Metrics

Growth accounting metrics are derived by combining different states into meaningful calculations that inform product strategy. Two key metrics that emerge from these combinations are:

1. **xAU** = New + Resurrected + Retained, where x is the abbreviation of time granularity
2. **Net growth** = New + Resurrected – Churned Users

These metrics are explained in the following sections:

xAU

When using the xAU metric, if we're measuring Daily Active Users (DAU), the x would be D for daily. Similarly, WAU represents Weekly Active Users, and MAU represents Monthly Active Users. This formula helps you to understand the composition of your active user base at any given time interval.

As shown in Figure 3-1, different transition states can be used to calculate the volume of your business units in active and inactive status. For example, Daily Active Users can be decomposed as follows:

DAU = D1 New + D1 Resurrected + D1 Retained

where

D1 New = Users who were new to the product today

D1 Resurrected = Users who resurrected for today

D1 Retained = Users who were in retained status for today

A general equation for active users is xAU = Dx New + Dx Resurrected + Dx Retained. In this equation, x represents the unit of time used to measure the active users, which can be daily, weekly, bi-weekly, monthly, or any other specified interval.

Net Growth

Net growth measures how many users you are growing/shrinking compared to yesterday.

DAU net growth = D1 New + D1 Resurrected − D1 Churned

where

D1 New = Users who were new to the product today

D1 Resurrected = Users who resurrected for today

D1 Churned = Users who were in churned status for today

Successful products should demonstrate consistent growth. This means that your net growth—the number of users you gained minus those lost—should be positive whether measured daily, weekly, or monthly.

However, it's important to recognize that positive net growth does not always indicate sustainable success. It can sometimes conceal underlying issues. For example, positive growth might occur simply because you invest heavily into acquiring new users (the "new" component), while existing users are leaving at an alarming rate.

UNDERSTANDING TRANSITIONS

To track these patterns accurately, compare user activity between two time periods: a previous window and a current window. It's like taking two snapshots of your user base and analyzing the differences. For instance, we classify a user as "resurrected" if they were inactive in the previous window but become active in the current window.

Nonoverlapping windows may seem like a logical approach. For example, one might assume monthly churn involves counting users who were active last month but inactive this month. However, this method does not accurately calculate churn in growth accounting.

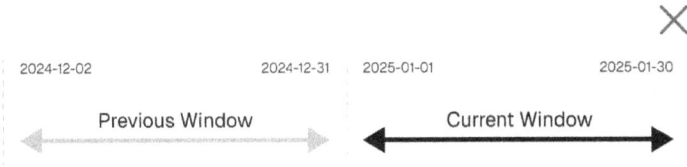

Figure 3-2: Nonoverlapping window illustration

Instead, growth accounting uses overlapping windows to accurately track user transitions. For example, when calculating monthly churn on January 31:

- **Previous window:** January 1–30
- **Current window:** January 2–31

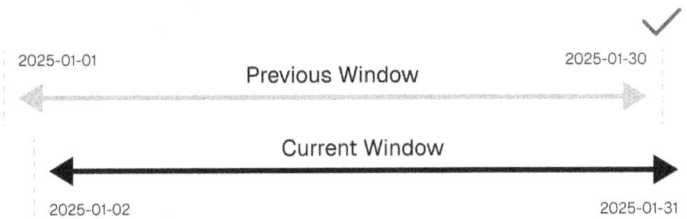

Figure 3-3: Overlapping window illustration

The overlapping approach captures daily changes in user behavior and aligns with the net growth equation. It provides a more accurate picture of user transitions by accounting for users who may be active at different points within the month, rather than just comparing two separate months.

Let's see how this works in practice.

Remember that MAU net growth (MAU today – MAU yesterday) = MAU new + MAU resurrected – MAU churned. Since this calculation measures daily changes in MAU, applying overlapping windows ensures accuracy.

Here's a practical example showing how to calculate MAU growth accounting states as of January 31, demonstrating the specific dates used for previous and current windows:

GROWTH ACCOUNTING STATE (AS OF JAN 31)	PREVIOUS WINDOW (JAN 1–JAN 30)	CURRENT WINDOW (JAN 2–JAN 31)
MAU New	Not acquired yet	Acquired
MAU Retained	Active	Active
MAU Churned	Active	Inactive
MAU Resurrected	Inactive	Active
MAU Stale	Inactive	Inactive

CASE STUDY

Let's examine a case study of MGA, a mobile gaming application that launched six months ago and is now focusing on growth.

KEY FRAMEWORK PARAMETERS

- **Unit of analysis:** Individual users
- **Active user definition:** Users who spend more than ten seconds playing a game
- **Time granularity:** Monthly Active Users (MAU) as the North Star metric

GROWTH ANALYSIS: JANUARY PERFORMANCE REVIEW

MAU Trend

MAU has grown significantly—up approximately 52 percent each week and quadrupling over the month. This represents strong growth. Let's decompose the MAU metric to understand which states have been driving this growth and what opportunities exist for further expansion.

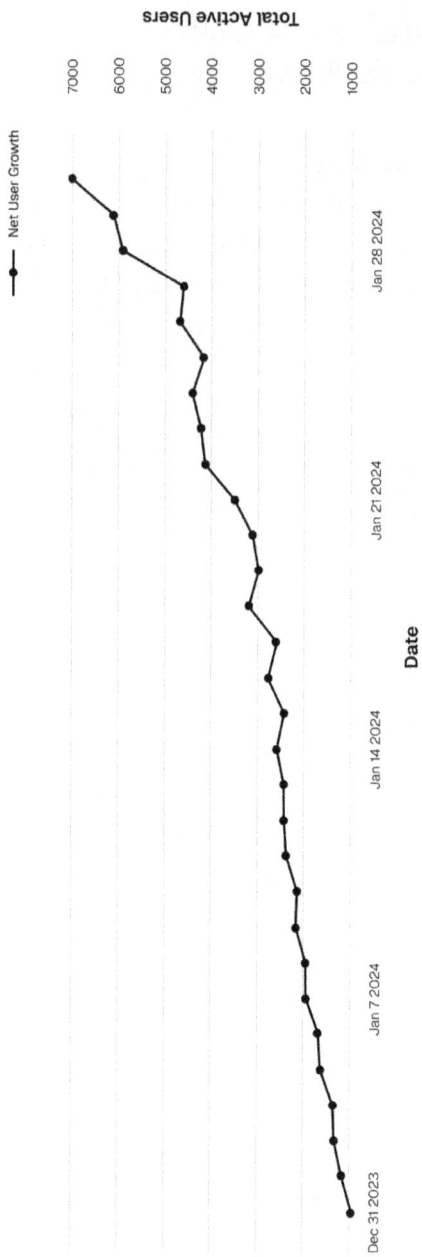

Figure 3-4: MAU trend

The following chart shows the breakdown of the MAU trend by different growth accounting buckets.

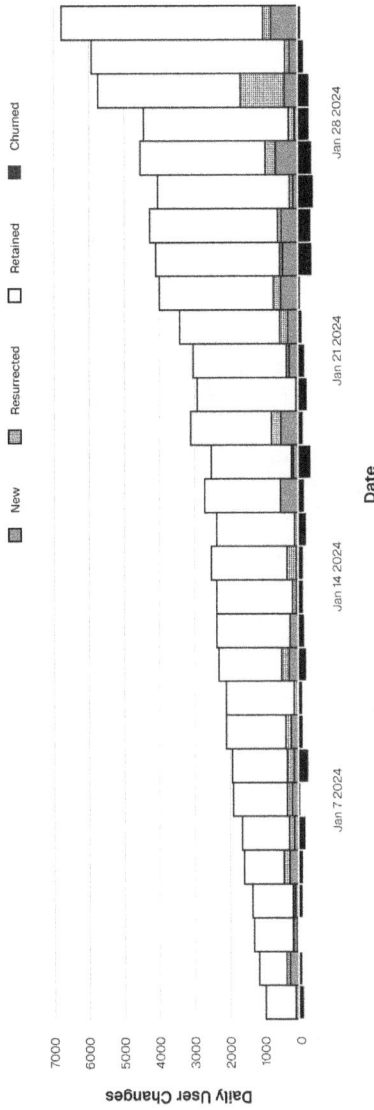

Figure 3-5: Detailed component trend analysis

1. New User Acquisition

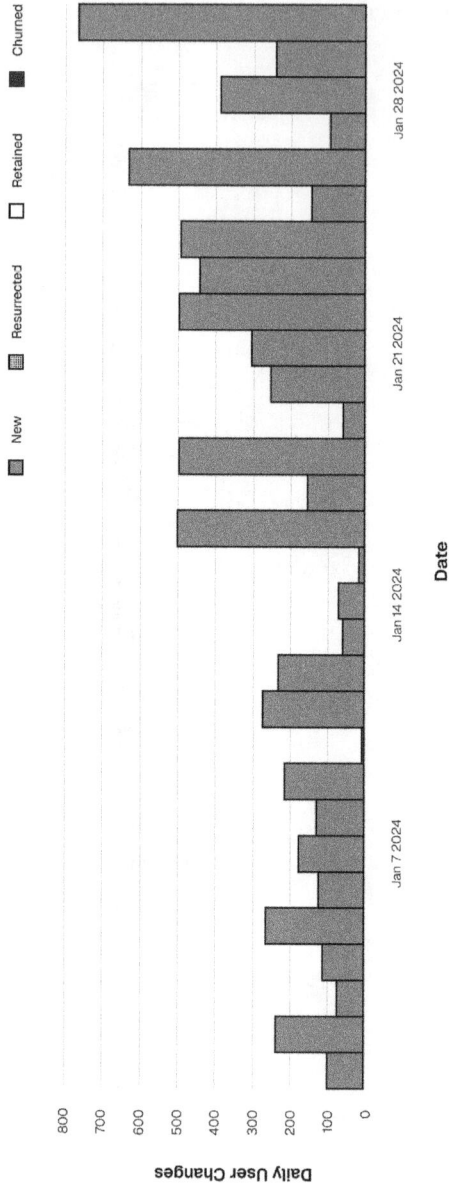

Figure 3-6: New user acquisition trend

- Notable dip on January 10.
- Initial slowdown in first two weeks.
- Significant acceleration post-January 21, coinciding with a new marketing campaign.

2. Churned User

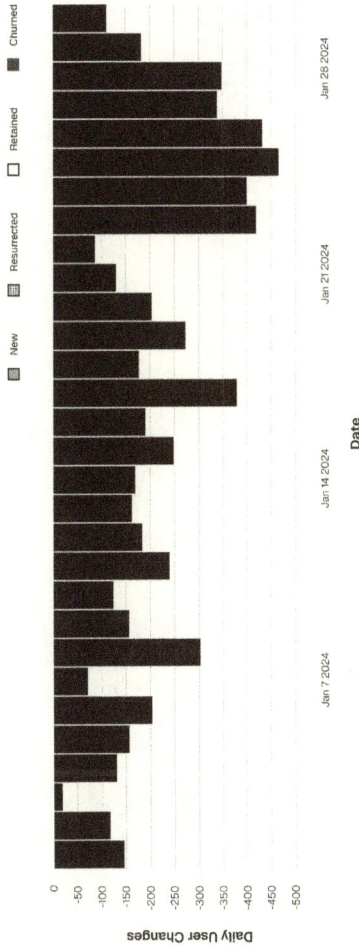

Figure 3-7: Churned user trend

- Elevated rates observed in late January.
- No correlation with seasonal events or holidays.
- Requires further investigation into root causes.

3. Resurrected User

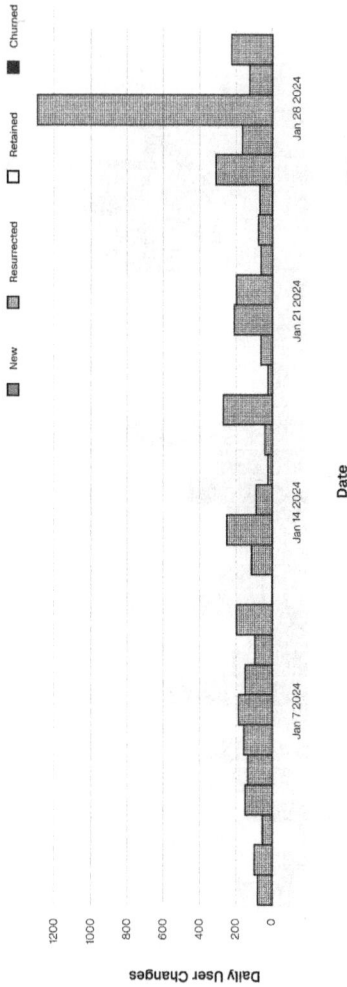

Figure 3-8: Resurrected user trend

- Major spike recorded on January 28.
- Success attributed to targeted notification strategy and marketing initiatives.

4. Retained User

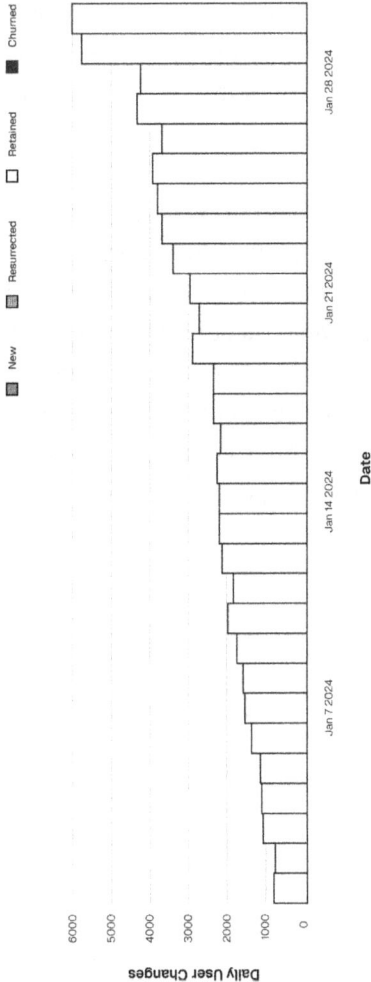

Figure 3-9: Retained user trend

- Initial plateau in mid-January.
- Strong acceleration in latter half of month.
- Overall positive trend indicating healthy user engagement.

After analyzing growth trends, the next question becomes which growth accounting category to prioritize to drive growth. While trend analysis provides valuable insights, the critical step involves developing and testing hypotheses about the causes of these trends and determining which hypotheses are feasible to pursue.

New users: New users grew 73 percent week-over-week (WoW) and doubled over the month. Analyzing the different market segments within the total addressable market for mobile gaming reveals that teens in Japan represent a promising market for user acquisition. Ads through Google and Meta launched on January 16, increasing awareness and downloads of the gaming app. After confirming these cohorts demonstrate strong retention, campaign spending can increase to acquire more users.

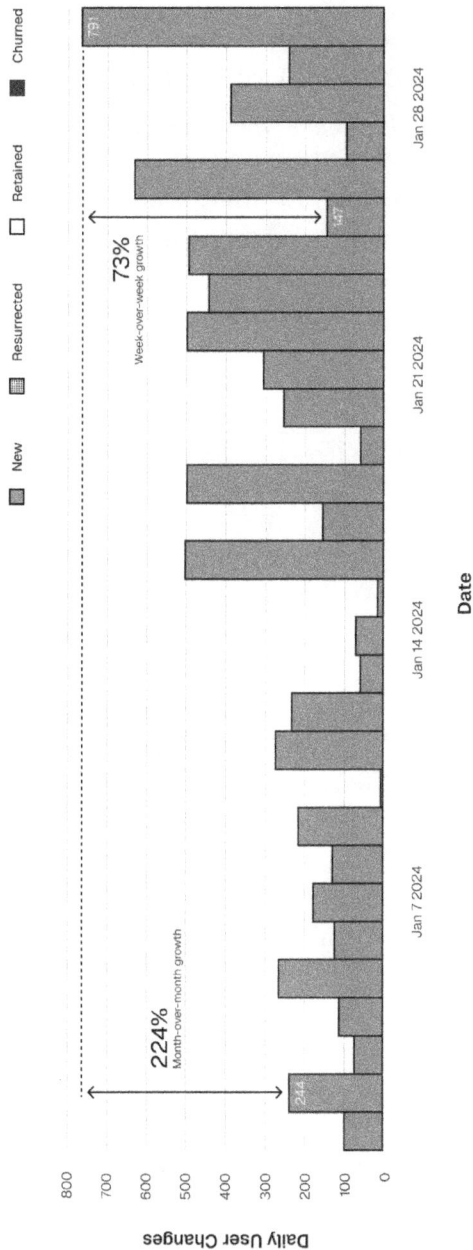

Figure 3-10: New user growth rate

Retained users: Retained users grew 62 percent WoW and six-fold over the month. If retained users occasionally trend down intermittently, it may indicate increasing churn over time. The app shows that retained users remained flat or trended down during specific periods. To ensure continuous growth in this metric, focus on enhancing user retention and engagement among retained users.

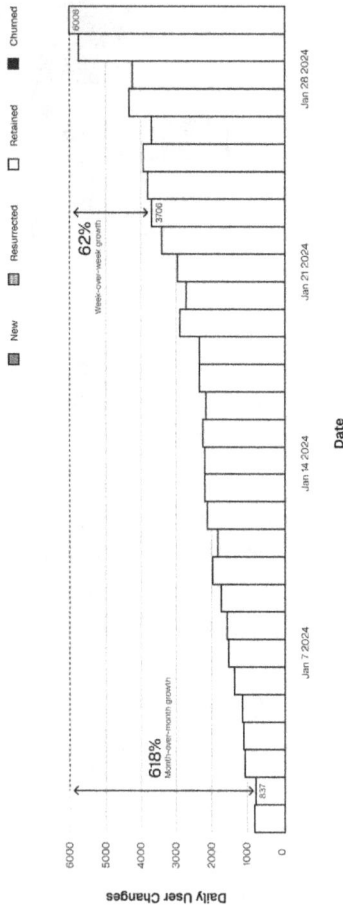

Figure 3-11: Retained user growth rate

Resurrected users: User resurrection increased by 251 percent week-over-week and nearly doubled over the month. The significant growth in resurrection last week resulted from a major spike on January 28, following the launch of new language translation features for Japanese teens. Notifications sent to this audience contributed to the spike.

Figure 3-12: Resurrected user growth rate

Churned users: To assess how bad churn is, we often look at net growth to begin with.

How is churn affecting my growth?

To understand the effect of churn, first examine net growth to determine whether it has been negative. Remember, net growth measures the change in the number of users compared to yesterday.

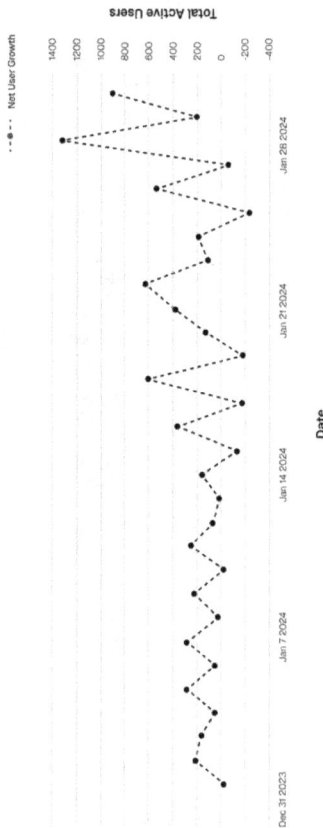

Figure 3-13: Net growth trend

Net growth consistently showed negative trends since mid-January but increased significantly during the last few days of the month. Now is the time to analyze the components of net growth to understand the impact of churn.

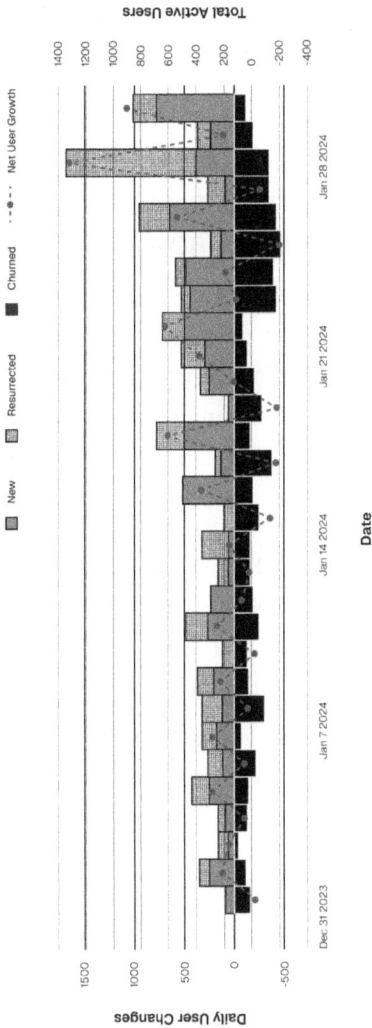

Figure 3-14: Trend of net growth components

Resurrections were significantly lower between January 15 to January 20 compared to churn, resulting in negative net growth. Churn rates also increased after January 23, primarily because the app lacked sufficient language support for Japanese users. As a result, many Japanese youth acquired during mid-January began to churn. However, following the launch of Japanese language support, many of the churned users resurrected on January 28.

GROWTH ACCOUNTING FRAMEWORK VARIATIONS
VARIATION 1: BUSINESS GROWTH ACCOUNTING

Traditional growth accounting primarily emphasizes active user metrics. However, an important variation applies this framework to revenue analysis. This approach enables businesses to understand the financial impact of user behavior patterns. See Chapter 7 for a detailed discussion.

VARIATION 2: SPECIALIZED GROWTH
STATE SEGMENTATION
Organic vs. Inorganic User Transitions

As products scale, they attract both legitimate users and potential bad actors, making it essential to distinguish between organic and inorganic user transitions. Inorganic churn occurs when users are deactivated due to:

- Detection of suspicious activity
- Identification of bot accounts
- Violations of policy

Monitoring inorganic churn is crucial for mature products to develop effective defense strategies. Users may temporarily enter an inorganic churn state while under investigation. If cleared, they transition to inorganic resurrection, which helps track false positive rates in integrity systems.

Voluntary vs. Nonvoluntary Churn in SaaS

In Software-as-a-Service (SaaS) businesses, understanding churn patterns requires distinguishing between voluntary decisions. Voluntary churn occurs when users actively choose to leave, such as a Netflix subscriber canceling due to perceived low value. Nonvoluntary churn may result from circumstances like:

- Payment processing failures
- Policy-related account suspensions
- Technical access issues

This distinction informs mitigation strategies: address voluntary churn with product improvements, and address nonvoluntary churn with operational solutions like better payment systems.

VARIATION 3: ENHANCED STATE DEFINITIONS

Growth accounting frameworks can be customized with additional granularity in active/inactive state definitions. When considering such modifications, ask:

"How will granular status distinctions impact business decisions and actions?"

Duolingo exemplifies this approach by incorporating "at risk" states into its user classification system.[2] Their framework distinguishes between Weekly Active Users (WAU) and Monthly Active Users (MAU) at risk of churning, which enables targeted engagement strategies.

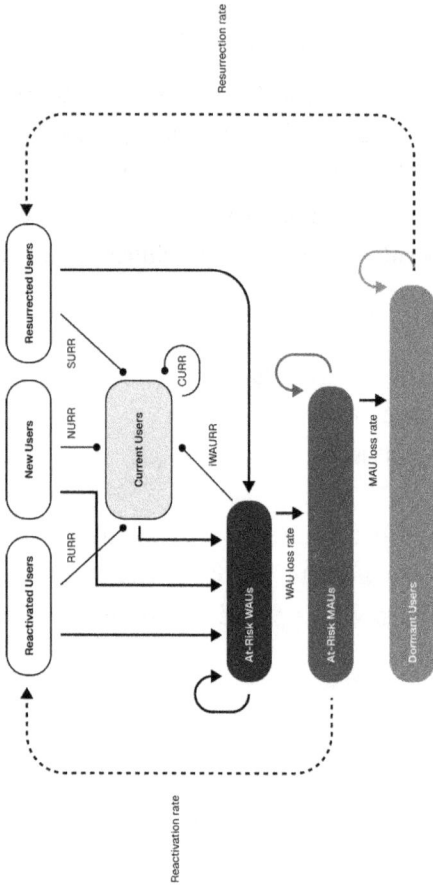

Figure 3-15: Duolingo growth model

---

2   Erin Gustafson, "Meaningful Metrics: How Data Sharpened the Focus of Product Teams," Duolingo blog, February 17, 2023, https://blog.duolingo.com/growth-model-duolingo/.

This granular approach allows Duolingo to implement specific gamification strategies for different user risk categories, demonstrating how enhanced state definitions can drive targeted intervention strategies.

TAKEAWAY

Growth accounting serves as a powerful framework that breaks down user growth into its core components, providing a comprehensive view of your product's health and growth dynamics. By analyzing user transitions between different statuses—from new to retained, churned to resurrected—you can identify the key drivers of your product's growth and areas needing attention.

To implement an effective growth accounting framework:

1. Define meaningful activity metrics that reflect genuine user value.
2. Map distinct user states and their transition status.
3. Systematically track state transitions.
4. Focus on the states that most significantly impact net growth.

The power of growth accounting lies in its ability to:

- Guide strategic decisions by revealing which user segments require attention, whether it's acquiring new users, retaining existing ones, or reengaging churned users.
- Provide actionable insights through historical trend analysis, enabling teams to evaluate the effectiveness of past initiatives and identify emerging challenges.

- Enable competitive benchmarking through standardized metrics like churn and resurrection rates.
- Offer a holistic view of product health that extends beyond individual metrics, ensuring balanced and sustainable growth.

EXERCISE
QUESTIONS

Question 1: Growth Detective—Solve the Mystery of App Growth 🔍

You are a data analyst at TrendyApp, a fast-growing social media platform. The CEO wants to understand what's happening with user growth. Here's the daily active user data:

METRIC	DAY 1	DAY 2
Total DAU	1000	1200
New Users	1000	300
Resurrected Users	0	100

Your Mission

1. Calculate the net user growth for day two (Hint: compare how many users were gained vs. lost).
2. What percentage of day two users are loyal (retained) users? Show your calculation method.
3. How many users churned on day two?

Bonus Challenge

What would you recommend to the CEO based on these
numbers? 🤔

Question 2: The User Journey Calendar 📅

Meet Alex, a user of FitTracker, a fitness app. Let's analyze
their engagement pattern.

Activity Timeline

1. January 1—Alex downloads and uses FitTracker for the
   first time. 🎉
2. January 2–7—Uses the app daily for workout tracking.
3. January 15—Returns after a break to log a gym session.
4. January 20, 28, 30, 31—Sporadic app usage.

Track Alex's User Status

1. Questions: Identify key transition dates:
   A. When did Alex become a WAU churned user?
   B. When did he resurrect?
   C. First appearance as DAU new?
   D. First DAU churn?
   E. First DAU retained?
2. Answers: Key transition dates:
   A. WAU churn: January 14
   B. WAU resurrection: January 15
   C. First DAU new: January 1
   D. First DAU churn: January 8
   E. First DAU retained: January 2

3. Status Check Points Questions:
   A. What was Alex's WAU status on January 20?
   B. Track the WAU journey on January 27 and January 28.
   C. Follow the DAU pattern on January 10, 30, and 31.
4. Answers: Status Check Points:
   A. January 20: WAU retained.
   B. January 27: WAU churn → January 28: WAU resurrected.
   C. January 10: DAU stale → January 30: DAU resurrected → January 31: DAU retained.

Chapter 4

ACQUIRE AND FOSTER HIGH-QUALITY USERS

INTRODUCTION: DRIVING SUSTAINABLE PRODUCT GROWTH

Sustainable growth of high-quality users is the lifeblood of any successful product. Without it, even the most innovative solutions can struggle to thrive in today's competitive landscape.

In a product's early days, organic growth through word of mouth often signals strong product market fit. Yet to scale effectively, teams must take a more strategic approach by identifying and targeting user segments that are most likely to discover, embrace, and derive lasting value from the product.

As growth accelerates, the composition of the user base inevitably evolves. Early adopters may give way to mainstream users, potentially diluting the overall user quality and introducing new segments with different needs and behaviors. This makes it crucial to understand and adapt to these changing dynamics, allowing teams to craft targeted strategies that nurture growth within their most valuable segments.

IDENTIFYING AND NURTURING HIGH-QUALITY USERS

In today's competitive market, sustainable growth hinges on attracting and retaining high-value users—those who not only engage deeply with our product but also contribute meaningfully to our business success. Understanding who these users are and what drives their behavior is crucial for optimizing both marketing efforts and product development.

KEY METRICS FOR MEASURING USER VALUE

We usually use three primary metrics to evaluate user quality:

1. Lifetime Value

Lifetime Value (LTV) measures the total revenue potential of a user throughout their relationship with our product. Using a basic calculation model (monthly revenue ÷ monthly churn rate, where churn rate represents the percentage of users who stop using the product each month), we can estimate a user's long-term value. For example, a user paying $10 monthly with a 10 percent churn rate (meaning 10 percent of users leave each month) has an estimated LTV of $100. While more sophisticated models exist, this baseline helps inform acquisition strategies.

However, LTV calculations become more reliable as products

mature and establish robust user attribution systems. For early stage products when we do not have enough history and data for the users, we often need to rely on other indicators.

2. Average Revenue per User

Average Revenue per User (ARPU) serves as an earlier indicator of user value, typically measured seven, fourteen, or thirty days post-sign up. It is calculated by dividing the total revenue generated during a specific period by the number of active users in that same period. For example, if a product generates $10,000 in revenue in a month with one thousand active users, the monthly ARPU would be $10. While it may not capture long-term behavior patterns or predict future revenue growth accurately, ARPU provides valuable initial insights into user monetization potential and helps teams make data-driven decisions about user acquisition and retention strategies.

3. Engagement and Retention Metrics

Beyond monetary metrics, we track behavioral indicators that often correlate with long-term value:

1. Time spent in product
2. Frequency of key actions (e.g., number of conversations in a chat app)
3. Short-term retention (two to three weeks post-sign up)
4. Long-term retention (six to twelve months post-sign up)

Understanding the user journey is equally important—how users progress from passive users to core users and ultimately become power users. This progression helps us identify opportunities to accelerate user growth and maximize value creation.

In the following sections, we'll explore how to leverage these insights to develop targeted marketing strategies and product optimizations that attract and nurture high-value users throughout their journey.

DISCOVERING YOUR IDEAL USERS: KEY SIGNALS FOR HIGH-QUALITY ACQUISITION

Now that we understand how to measure user quality through key metrics like LTV, ARPU, and engagement, let's explore how to identify and attract these high-value users. By analyzing pre-sign up signals and behaviors, we can develop targeted acquisition strategies that resonate with our ideal user segments.

1. Geographic location/locale
   A. **Hypothesis:** Users from certain regions consistently demonstrate higher conversion rates and lifetime value, influenced by market dynamics, purchasing power, and product market fit.
   B. **Implication:** Focus marketing efforts and localization strategies on high-performing regions.
2. Device and browser information
   A. **Hypothesis:** Device preferences and browser choices often reveal user sophistication and conversion likelihood. Multidevice users typically show stronger engagement and retention patterns.
   B. **Implication:** Optimize the product experience for devices and browsers favored by high-value users, and

promote cross-platform usage by encouraging desktop users to download the mobile app.

3. Page visit or app navigation patterns
   A. **Hypothesis:** High-intent users exhibit distinct browsing patterns, often deeply exploring pricing, features, and documentation pages before converting.
   B. **Implication:** Optimize these key pages or app navigation flow and create clear paths to them from entry points.

4. Time spent on site
   A. **Hypothesis:** Extended site exploration strongly correlates with higher interest and conversion potential.
   B. **Implication:** Create engaging content and clear navigation paths to keep potential high-value users on the site longer.

STRATEGIES FOR HIGH-QUALITY USER ACQUISITION
1. ORGANIC GROWTH: THE FOUNDATION

The most valuable users often come through organic channels, driven by compelling features and intuitive product experiences that naturally encourage word-of-mouth sharing. For a deeper exploration of this approach, see the section on Product-Led Growth (PLG) in Chapter 7.

2. VIRAL LOOP: AMPLIFYING GROWTH THROUGH USER NETWORKS

A **viral loop** transforms your product into a self-propagating growth engine, where existing users naturally bring in new users—creating sustainable expansion with minimal marketing investment.

Let's explore three powerful viral loop strategies:

1. **Explicit incentive-based:** Think of traditional referral programs where users receive tangible rewards for bringing others to the platform. Each successful referral creates a new ambassador, perpetuating the growth cycle.
2. **Direct feature-enabled:** The product itself necessitates user expansion. Consider chat apps—their core functionality requires users to invite others, creating natural network effects.
3. **Indirect user acquisition:** This sophisticated approach leverages product interactions to capture potential user contacts. For example, when a calendar app user schedules a meeting with nonusers, it creates opportunities for targeted outreach and feature-gated experiences that drive sign-ups.

Measuring Viral Success Through Analytics
Viral Coefficient Analysis:

The virality coefficient K is our North Star metric for measuring viral growth, where K = number of viral users ÷ number of nonviral users.

A virality coefficient of 0.05 represents the threshold for sustainable viral growth—meaning every one hundred existing users bring in five new ones. This metric guides optimization efforts: if virality falls short, teams can enhance referral incentives or streamline the invitation process.

However, interpret this metric carefully. For instance, while our K value improved from 0.01 in March to 0.05 in June, this could reflect either enhanced viral mechanisms or a decrease in nonviral acquisition—highlighting the importance of contextual analysis for any ratio-based metrics.

Daily virality factor K = viral instances / non-viral instances

7-day moving avg

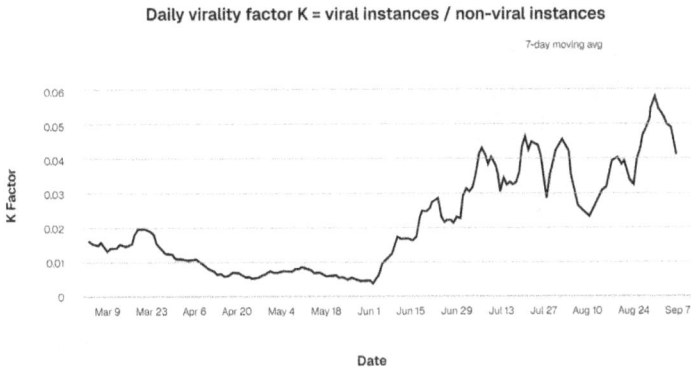

Figure 4-1: Virality factor trend

Cost-Benefit Analysis

For referral programs and campaigns, striking the right balance is crucial. The incentive must be compelling enough to drive new user acquisition while maintaining profitability. This requires careful analysis of customer acquisition cost (CAC) versus lifetime value (LTV). Beyond monetary incentives, the focus should always be on attracting users who show strong potential for long-term product success.

3. PAID CAMPAIGNS AND PROGRAMS

Strategic paid campaigns can be a powerful tool for reaching potential customers through optimal distribution channels. While paid campaign analytics deserves its own comprehensive discussion, here are key strategies for success:

- **Use look-alike audiences:** Leverage platforms like Facebook or Google Ads to target users who share characteristics with your most successful customers.
- **Target high-intent keywords:** Focus on search terms that signal clear purchase intent or specific pain points your product addresses.
- **A/B test creatives and messaging:** Continuously refine your campaigns to resonate with users who demonstrate the right motivation and intent.
- **Create paid programs for high-value customers:** Implement targeted programs, such as startup initiatives, offering strategic discounts or trials. These programs help accelerate adoption, enhance retention, and foster growth alongside your customers' success.

4. NONPAID MARKETING EFFORTS

Beyond paid channels, a robust marketing strategy includes SEO optimization targeting high-value customer search terms, engaging webinars, and community-building events. Strategic keyword competitor analysis reveals opportunities to enhance content and attract premium users. This comprehensive approach ensures sustainable growth through multiple channels.

SEGMENTING USER TRAFFIC: UNDERSTANDING DIFFERENT USER JOURNEYS

The types of market segmentation analysis

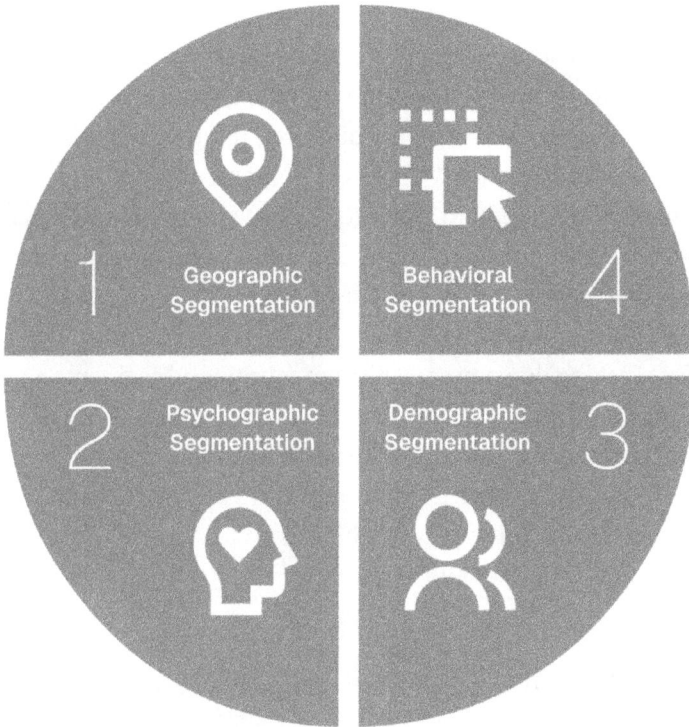

Figure 4-2: Traffic segmentation

Think of your product as a bustling city, where different types of visitors navigate its streets with varying purposes and destinations. Some are like tourists, briefly exploring before moving on. Others are potential residents, carefully evaluating whether to make your product their digital home. But the most valuable visitors—your high-quality users—are like those who not only settle in but actively contribute to the city's vibrancy and growth.

As discussed in a previous chapter on product market fit, understanding user friction points is crucial. Just as a city might have confusing street signs or poorly lit areas that deter visitors, products often have hidden barriers that prevent adoption. A notable case study from a fast-growing startup revealed that users who encountered difficulties with core features in their first week were 70 percent more likely to abandon the product. However, those who successfully navigated these initial challenges were three times more likely to become long-term, high-value customers.

By breaking down user traffic into meaningful segments and identifying these friction points early, teams can remove obstacles and create smoother pathways that resonate with potential high-value users' needs. Let's explore several key segmentation categories that help us understand and nurture these valuable user journeys.

UNDERSTANDING FRICTION POINTS IN YOUR PRODUCT'S PRE-LANDING JOURNEY

A funnel is the strategic pathway users follow, transforming curious visitors into engaged users. Like a master architect designing a grand entrance, understanding these funnels is essential for crafting an experience that not only welcomes users but guides them effortlessly toward their goals. For our AI-powered chat application, the registration funnel serves as this critical first impression. Let's dissect this sophisticated journey:

Step 1—Landing Page Visit: The gateway opens as users discover our platform through diverse channels—whether through targeted advertising campaigns, organic search results, or powerful word-of-mouth referrals.

Step 2—Registration Form: At this crucial touchpoint, users establish their digital presence by providing key credentials—a unique email identifier, distinctive username, and secure password, complemented by optional profile enrichments.

Step 3—Email Verification: Security meets seamlessness as we deploy a sophisticated verification system, sending a secure link or verification code to authenticate user identity.

Step 4—Account Activation: The transformation occurs as users complete their verification, crossing the threshold from visitor to verified member through a streamlined activation process.

Step 5—Profile Setup: Users breathe life into their digital presence, crafting a personalized experience through thoughtful profile customization and preference configuration.

Step 6—Welcome Message: The journey culminates in an elegant onboarding experience, where users discover platform capabilities through an intuitive tutorial that seamlessly introduces core features and community standards.

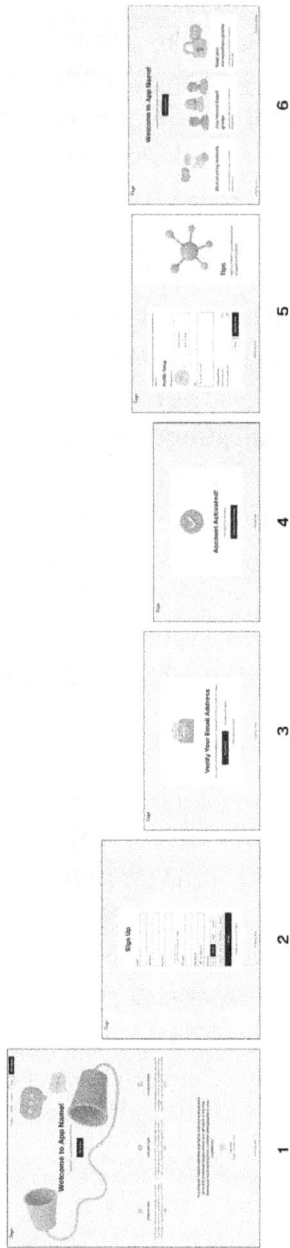

Figure 4-3: Sign-up funnel illustration

104 · GROWTH DATA ANALYTICS PLAYBOOK

By analyzing drop-off points in this funnel, teams can identify critical improvements. For instance, high abandonment during email verification might signal the need for streamlined authentication, such as implementing single sign-on with Google or Apple accounts.

KEY PERFORMANCE INDICATORS

There are two key metrics to understand the funnel.

User counts: Track completion numbers at each funnel stage

Conversion rates: Measure the percentage of users advancing through each step.

What follows is an example of how these metrics look:

STEP	STEP NAME	USER COUNT	CONVERSION RATE
1	Landing Page Visit	100	
2	Registration Form	90	90 percent
3	Email Verification	55	55 percent
4	Account Activation	30	30 percent
5	Profile Setup	20	20 percent
6	Welcome Message	19	19 percent

Table 4-1: Example data for the sign-up funnel

Sign-up funnel analysis

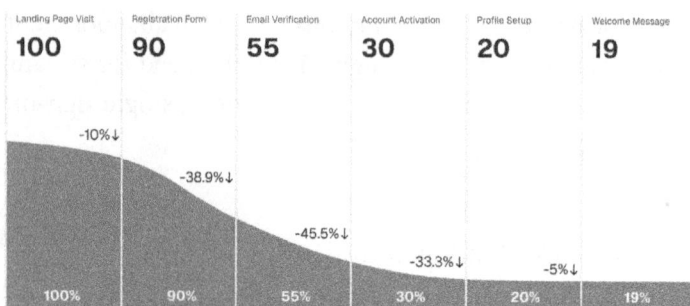

Landing Page Visit	Registration Form	Email Verification	Account Activation	Profile Setup	Welcome Message
100	**90**	**55**	**30**	**20**	**19**

-10%↓

-38.9%↓

-45.5%↓

-33.3%↓

-5%↓

| 100% | 90% | 55% | 30% | 20% | 19% |

Figure 4-4: Sign-up funnel metrics for old sign-up flow

After implementing single sign-on, we saw a dramatic transformation in our funnel metrics. The simplified authentication process removed a major friction point, leading to these impressive numbers:

STEP	STEP NAME	USER COUNT	CONVERSION RATE
1	Landing Page Visit	100	
2	Registration Form	90	90 percent
3	Single Sign-in Registration	80	80 percent
4	Profile Setup	60	60 percent
5	Welcome Message	58	58 percent

Table 4-2: User onboarding funnel analysis

Landing Page Visit	Registration Form	Single Sign-On Registration	Profile Setup	Welcome Message
100	**90**	**80**	**60**	**58**

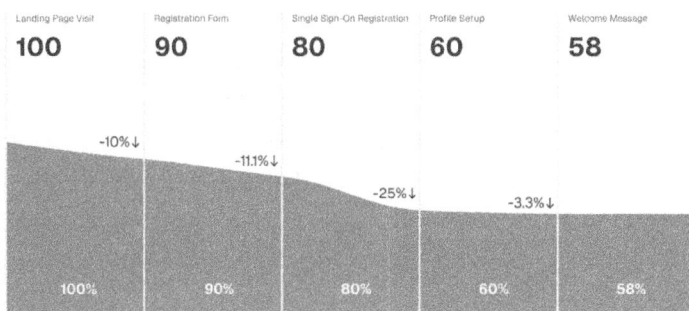

-10%↓   -11.1%↓   -25%↓   -3.3%↓

100%   90%   80%   60%   58%

Figure 4-5: Sign-up funnel metrics for modified sign-up flow

Caveats

Optimizing the funnel solely for completion rate is not always the best strategy.

Let me share a story from our early days of a gaming product. We noticed users abandoning the platform during profile setup. The easiest solution would have been to remove this step entirely. However, we retained it because users are most motivated to provide essential information during initial setup. Instead of removing the step, we introduced targeted incentives like "complete your profile to unlock premium features" and added an engaging guided tour. Our completion rates improved dramatically. However, it's a delicate balance. While we aim to create a smooth journey, certain checkpoints serve as valuable filters. Netflix, for example, requires credit card information before users can start a trial. Though this creates friction, it effectively ensures committed users. This strategic friction helps distinguish serious users from casual browsers.

OPTIMIZING FIRST-TIME USER EXPERIENCE AND PRODUCT VALUE DISCOVERY

First impressions are crucial for new users—this is when their curiosity and motivation to learn about your product are at their peak. The key challenge lies in helping users quickly grasp the product's value in their daily lives. To achieve this, we must continuously refine the new user experience to help users form a strong connection with the product from day one.

Facebook's success story provides an excellent example. They discovered that adding friends in the first few days—especially friends who have content on their timeline—is crucial for users' long-term engagement. This insight led them to reshape their landing experience around connecting users with friends and suggesting connections through "Friends You May Know."

How can we identify the features or actions that make users truly value our product? The answer lies in studying our existing high-quality users and their behavior patterns. By analyzing their journey, particularly during their early days with the product, we can pinpoint specific features that strongly correlate with long-term retention and engagement. A simple approach is to examine how users interact with features during their first session or day. By comparing patterns between low- and high-quality users, we can understand how these behaviors relate to long-term retention or conversion. For instance, if data shows that users who enable subtitles in a video app are more likely to stay, you can highlight this feature during the onboarding tour.

Segmentation and funnels should be used together to narrow

down the focus. For example, if you find that users from a particular country consistently have the highest drop-off on one of the onboarding pages, you can test whether the question has different cultural implications and should be presented differently for that country's users.

The basic framework for identifying growth opportunity areas is:

- The segment(s)/steps that have high volume but low high-quality conversion rate
  - For these segments, we should focus on how to drive their conversion.
- The segment(s)/steps that have high conversion rate but low volume
  - For these segments, we should focus on how to drive top-of-funnel acquisition.
- The segment(s)/steps that have medium-level performance in either traffic or conversion but have shown steady growth in either dimension

TAKEAWAY

In this chapter, we discussed how to identify the high-value users and how to leverage marketing and product strategies to further our acquisition along with making users understand the value of the product faster.

Based on users' journey with the product, there are three key stages where you can achieve these goals:

1. **Pre-sign up:** Identify quality indicators through geo-

graphic location, device usage, page visit patterns, and time spent metrics. Achieve higher marketing ROI through better-targeted marketing efforts.

2. **Onboarding flow/registration funnel:** Analyze and optimize various funnels to improve user conversion while maintaining user quality and gathering essential user information.

3. **First landing experience:** Study successful users to understand how they find the product valuable to them and their critical engagement patterns, then promote key features to drive long-term engagement.

EXERCISE

Background: The game has different user segments based on their acquisition channels: organic, paid social media, and app store ads. Here's their funnel data for the past month:

CHANNEL	DOWNLOADS	SIGN-UPS	TUTORIAL COMPLETE	DAY 1 RETENTION	DAY 7 RETENTION
Organic	10,000	8,000	6,000	45 percent	28 percent
Paid Social	50,000	35,000	20,000	25 percent	12 percent
App Store Ads	25,000	20,000	15,000	35 percent	20 percent

Table 4-3: User acquisition funnel performance by marketing channel

ADDITIONAL DATA

1. The average cost per install (CPI) is $2.50 for paid social and $3.50 for app store ads.

2. Users who complete the tutorial are three times more likely to make in-app purchases.

3. The game monetizes through in-app purchases, with an average revenue per paying user of $15.

QUESTIONS

Question 1: Which acquisition channel shows the highest-quality users? Support your answer with data.

Question 2: Calculate the conversion rate from download to tutorial completion for each channel. What insights can you draw?

Question 3: If you had an additional $100,000 marketing budget, how would you allocate it between paid social and app store ads? Explain your reasoning using the provided metrics.

Question 4: What specific recommendations would you make to improve the tutorial completion rate for the paid social channel?

Bonus Challenge: Create a simple ROI calculation for each paid channel, considering the CPI, conversion rates, and average revenue per paying user.

ANSWERS

Question 1: Which acquisition channel shows the highest-quality users? Support your answer with data.

Answer: Highest-Quality Users. Organic users show the highest quality because:

- Highest Day 1 retention (45 percent) and Day 7 retention (28 percent)
- Best tutorial completion rate (60 percent vs. 40 percent for paid social and 60 percent for app store)
- Zero acquisition cost

Question 2: Calculate the conversion rate from download to tutorial completion for each channel. What insights can you draw?

Answer: Conversion Rates (Download to Tutorial)

- Organic: 60 percent (6,000/10,000)
- Paid Social: 40 percent (20,000/50,000)
- App Store Ads: 60 percent (15,000/25,000)
- Insight: Paid social users have significantly lower engagement, suggesting potential targeting issues or misaligned user expectations.

Question 3: If you had an additional $100,000 marketing budget, how would you allocate it between paid social and app store ads? Explain your reasoning using the provided metrics.

Answer: Budget Allocation. The recommendation is to allocate $70,000 to app store ads and $30,000 to paid social, Reasoning:

- App store ads show better retention rates (35 percent D1 vs. 25 percent for paid social).

- Higher tutorial completion rate (60 percent vs. 40 percent).
- Though CPI is higher ($3.50 vs. $2.50), the quality metrics justify the cost.

Question 4: What specific recommendations would you make to improve the tutorial completion rate for the paid social channel?

Answer: Recommendations for paid social:

- Improve ad targeting to match organic user profiles.
- Add pre-tutorial content in ads to set proper expectations.
- A/B test different ad creatives focusing on gameplay.
- Implement social features early in the tutorial.
- Consider shorter tutorial versions for social media-acquired users.

Bonus Challenge: Create a simple ROI calculation for each paid channel, considering the CPI, conversion rates, and average revenue per paying user.

Answer:

- Paid Social
  - Cost per 1,000 users: $2,500
  - Tutorial completion: 400 users (40 percent)
  - Estimated paying users (three times more likely): 120
  - Revenue: 120 × $15 = $1,800
  - ROI = ($1,800 – $2,500) ÷ $2,500 = –28 percent
- App Store:
  - Cost per 1,000 users: $3,500

- Tutorial completion: 600 users (60 percent)
- Estimated paying users (three times more likely): 180
- Revenue: 180 × $15 = $2,700
- ROI = ($2,700 – $3,500) ÷ $3,500 = –23 percent

Chapter 5

RETAIN EXISTING USERS AND KEEP THEM ENGAGED

After successfully acquiring high-quality users and demonstrating your product's value, the next crucial challenge is to transform these users into devoted advocates who consistently engage with your product. Let's explore how to make your product an indispensable part of their daily routine.

UNDERSTANDING STICKINESS AND RETENTION: TWO PILLARS OF USER ENGAGEMENT

As we explored in Chapter 2, product market fit (PMF) serves as the foundation of sustainable growth. While PMF emphasizes creating value that resonates with your target market, stickiness and retention metrics validate and quantify that fit by measuring how effectively your product keeps users engaged over time. These metrics build upon the initial PMF indicators we discussed earlier, providing deeper insights into how well your product maintains its market position and delivers consistent value to users.

Stickiness measures how frequently users actively engage with your product, typically within a month. It serves as a powerful indicator of your product's ability to become embedded in users' daily routines. Think of stickiness as the "habit factor"—the extent to which users incorporate your product into their regular activities. When users interact with your product, whether daily, weekly, or monthly, these touchpoints create patterns that reveal the strength of their engagement.

> 💡 High stickiness is a strong predictor of long-term success. When users frequently return to your product without any prompts, it signals that they have found genuine value that keeps them coming back. This natural, habitual usage is far more powerful than engagement driven by external reminders or incentives.

Retention, while related to stickiness, examines a different aspect of user behavior. It measures your product's ability to maintain its user base over time, often through strategic initiatives like notifications, reminders, and targeted campaigns. You can measure retention across different time horizons—from short-term (WAU@day14) to long-term (MAU@day90)—providing a comprehensive view of user loyalty.

The key distinction lies in the focus: **retention** assesses whether your users remain over time, while **stickiness** evaluates how often users use your product when they do stay. In other words, retention assigns a binary flag (0 or 1) and counts the ratio of 1s, while stickiness measures intraday usage by taking a numeric value.

A sticky product delivers such a compelling experience that users return naturally, motivated by the consistent value they receive. This organic engagement is especially important for products designed for frequent use, as it indicates sustainable, long-term adoption.

💡 Stickiness may not be the most meaningful engagement metric for seasonal products, such as tax-filing applications.

STICKINESS RETENTION FRAMEWORK

Now, let's explore a powerful framework that illustrates the relationship between stickiness and retention, revealing essential insights about your product's position and strategic priorities. To use the stickiness retention framework, first assess your product's stickiness by measuring user engagement frequency and satisfaction over time. Next, analyze retention metrics across different time horizons to identify patterns that enhance user loyalty and drive sustainable growth.

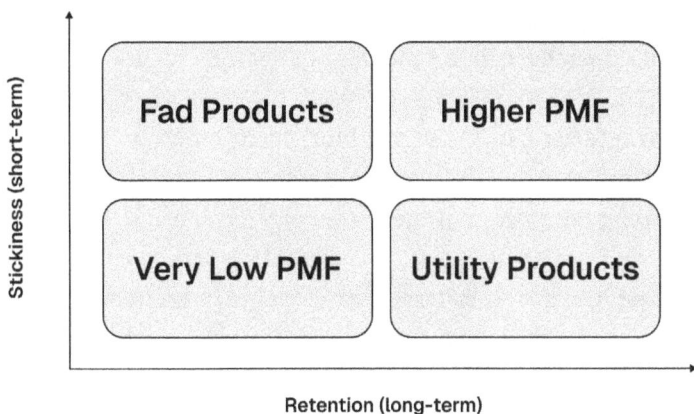

Figure 5-1: Product market fit insights: retention vs. stickiness matrix

Each of the four quadrants in the stickiness retention framework is described in detail:

Quadrant One. The Gold Standard: High Stickiness and High Retention

Example products: Instagram and Slack have mastered the art of becoming daily essentials, seamlessly woven into users' routines.

Characteristics: These products embody the ideal of user engagement—frequent, meaningful interactions paired with lasting loyalty. Users do not just visit; they make these products integral to their digital lives.

Focus: The challenge lies in pursuing strategic growth while preserving the unique appeal that keeps users returning.

Quadrant Two. The Shooting Star: High Stickiness and Low Retention

Example products: Consider viral mobile games or trending social apps that capture intense but fleeting attention.

Characteristics: These products burn brightly, but fade quickly. Users initially become hooked, spending hours daily, but their enthusiasm wanes as novelty diminishes.

Focus: The goal is to transform temporary excitement into lasting value through continuous innovation and deeper user engagement.

Quadrant Three. The Reliable Partner:
Low Stickiness and High Retention

Example products: TurboTax exemplifies this category—it's not used daily, but remains irreplaceable when needed.

Characteristics: These products address crucial but occasional needs, securing user loyalty through consistent reliability rather than frequent engagement.

Focus: The opportunity lies in expanding value through complementary services while maintaining the core trusted relationship.

Quadrant Four. The Warning Sign: Low
Stickiness and Low Retention

Example products: These are products struggling to find their audience or deliver clear value.

Characteristics: When users neither engage regularly nor stay, it's a clear indication that fundamental product market fit is missing.

Focus: It's probably time for a candid reassessment and bold action to redefine the product's value proposition and user experience.

THE POWER OF DAU/MAU: YOUR NORTH STAR FOR USER ENGAGEMENT

The DAU/MAU ratio is the gold standard for measuring product stickiness. This metric reveals the percentage of your Monthly Active Users who engage with your product daily, offering clear insights into user engagement patterns. For example, if a product gets one thousand daily users out of five thousand monthly users, it achieves a DAU/MAU ratio of 20 percent, indicating a significant potential for deeper user engagement.

The true power of DAU/MAU lies in its versatility. While it provides a broad overview at the product level, segmentation reveals its true potential. By analyzing this ratio across different user demographics and acquisition channels, you can uncover hidden patterns that drive engagement. Use these insights as your guide to optimize everything from marketing strategies to onboarding experiences.

ADAPTING DAU/MAU FOR YOUR PRODUCT REALITY

Not all products are created equal, and their engagement metrics should reflect this diversity. Tailor your measurement approach as follows:

- **High-frequency products:** For social media platforms and messaging apps, prioritize daily engagement. A strong DAU/MAU ratio acts as your pulse check for user habits and product stickiness.
- **Moderate-frequency products:** For project management tools and financial apps, use WAU/MAU (Weekly Active Users/Monthly Active Users) to better align with natural usage patterns, providing deeper insights.
- **Low-frequency products:** Travel platforms and e-commerce sites benefit from tracking MAU/TAU (Monthly Active Users/Total Active Users). This ratio

reveals market penetration and resurrection opportunities for reengagement. For example, if you have six hundred users in a one thousand-user market but only 20 percent maintain monthly engagement, you've identified a prime opportunity to reengage dormant users.

This stickiness metric has become the industry standard, prominently featured in financial reports of leading tech companies. Its simplicity and effectiveness in measuring user engagement make it an essential tool for product teams worldwide.

KEY APPLICATIONS

- **Performance benchmarking:** Many companies report their DAU and MAU metrics, making it easier to benchmark stickiness across industries. For example, leading social media and communication platforms achieve DAU/MAU ratios of 50 percent or higher, demonstrating exceptional user engagement. In contrast, e-commerce and content platforms typically demonstrate healthy ratios between 20–30 percent, reflecting their distinct usage patterns.
- **Predictive power:** DAU/MAU serves as a powerful leading indicator of long-term retention, particularly for high-frequency products like gaming apps. However, its predictive value varies by product type. While DAU/MAU proves critical for daily-use applications, it may lose relevance for seasonal or utility-focused products like tax-filing services.

MASTERING USER ACTIVITY METRICS: L/W/MNESS FRAMEWORK

The L/W/Mness framework offers a sophisticated yet intuitive approach for measuring user engagement across varying time horizons. This versatile suite of metrics enables product teams to analyze user behavior patterns and make data-driven decisions that enhance engagement.

UNDERSTANDING LNESS: THE DAILY ENGAGEMENT METRIC

Lness measures the number of active days within a specified period L, offering a precise measure of user engagement intensity. For example, using L30 (thirty-day window), if a user is active for twenty-five days, their L30 value is twenty-five. This indicates the user demonstrates significantly higher engagement compared to a user who is active for only five days. This detailed perspective helps you to identify your most valuable users and pinpoint those at risk of churning.

BEYOND DAILY METRICS: WNESS AND MNESS

The framework adapts to various product usage frequencies:

Weekly Activity (Wness)

For products designed for weekly interactions, such as learning platforms or fitness apps:

- Measures active weeks over a defined period (For example, W8 tracks activity over eight weeks).
- Identifies engagement trends and predicts user success

(For example, users with W8 less than three may need intervention).

Monthly Activity (Mness)

This framework is suitable for products with longer engagement cycles:

- Analyzes patterns over extended periods (For example, M6 examines six-month engagement).
- Provides valuable insights for seasonal businesses to understand cyclical trends.

Building on our understanding of Wness and Mness metrics, let's explore practical strategies to enhance engagement across various time horizons. While these metrics help us measure user activity patterns, the following approaches can help transform occasional users into regular participants, whether they engage weekly or monthly:

- **Achievement-based motivation:** "Level up your skills! 📚 Complete today's lesson to earn your Advanced Certificate." "✨ Impressive fourteen-day streak! You're close to joining our Top Learners Circle."
- **Targeted reengagement:** "Ready to continue your learning journey? Enjoy a special forty-eight-hour offer: 30 percent off all courses! 🚀"

KEY APPLICATIONS

Strategic user segmentation: Transform raw engagement data into actionable insights by segmenting your user base into distinct categories:

- Power Champions (L30 > 25): Your most dedicated users who drive product growth and innovation
- Core Users (L30 between 10–24): The steady backbone of your user community
- Growth Opportunities (L30 < 10): Users with untapped potential for deeper engagement

By analyzing these segments across regions and acquisition channels, you will uncover patterns that reveal your most effective growth strategies and identify markets where your product resonates most strongly. This intelligence becomes invaluable for crafting targeted campaigns and optimizing user experiences. We'll explore the captivating world of power users in detail in the next section.

Proactive churn prevention: Stay ahead of user attrition by monitoring engagement trends. When you notice declining activity patterns across Lness, Wness, or Mness metrics, seize the opportunity for timely intervention. This early warning system enables you to reengage users before they fully disengage, helping you maintain healthy user retention rates.

POWER USERS: YOUR PRODUCT'S MOST VALUABLE CHAMPIONS

The concept of power users is everywhere. Let us look at a study of alcohol drinks in the United States. Figure 5-2 is a histogram of how frequent people drink by decile.

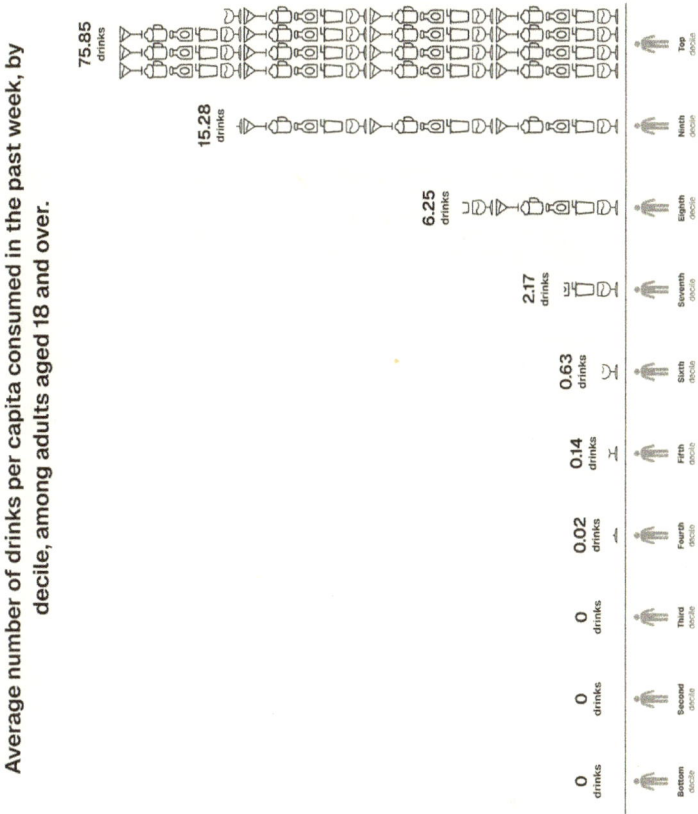

Figure 5-2: Histogram of alcohol consumption for adults in the United States

The median American consumes little alcohol, while only a small percentage drinks significantly more. Power laws generally apply in consumer products, revealing a common pattern:

roughly 10 percent of users account for about 90 percent of all product engagement. Power users are those who engage with a product at exceptional levels, and understanding them is crucial for product success.

You can measure this engagement in various ways, with Lness serving as a preferred metric. When analyzing the Lness distribution of users over the past month—ranked from lowest to highest activity—look for spikes in activity patterns or set a threshold where users above a specific Lness value represent 80 percent of total activity. Although these thresholds may seem arbitrary, the graph that follows illustrates that users with an Lness above twenty generate the majority of engagement.

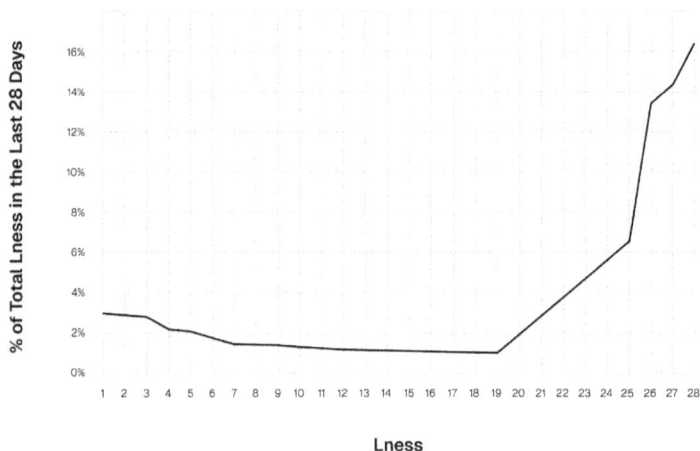

Figure 5-3: Distribution of Lness in the last twenty-eight days

The cumulative Lness graph shows that users with twenty or more active days account for 70 percent of total activity, indicating that twenty days is a sensible threshold for identifying power users.

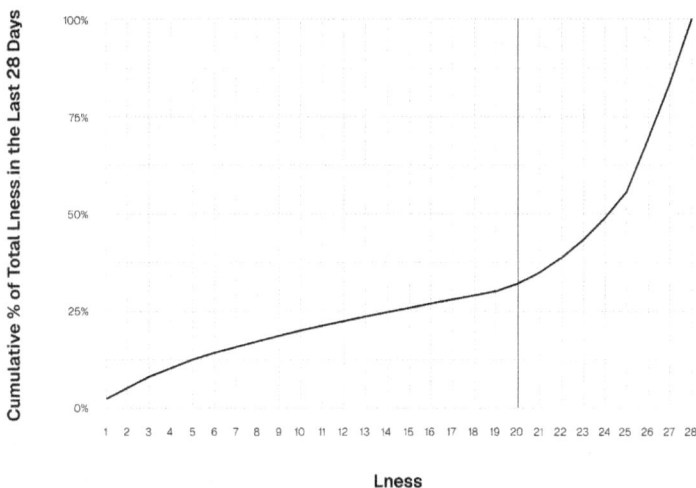

Figure 5-4: Cumulative Lness graph

Understanding power users is essential for product success. Identifying and analyzing these super-users can significantly transform your product strategy. Here's how:

- **Unlock growth patterns:** Study the behaviors of power users to decode the DNA of successful product adoption. Create a road map to elevate casual users into devoted advocates.
- **Drive product innovation:** Power users test your product's limits, serving as living laboratories for feature development. They reveal opportunities that could revolutionize your product experience.
- **Supercharge marketing ROI:** Understand where and how you acquire power users to replicate your success. Target look-alike audiences with precision to maximize marketing effectiveness.
- **Boost bottom line:** Power users are not only active;

they're also profitable. Their higher usage rates and adoption of premium features drive sustainable revenue growth.

- **Amplify product voice:** These users become your most authentic brand ambassadors, providing invaluable word-of-mouth marketing and deep insights that guide product evolution.
- **Strengthen network effects:** In multiplayer products, power users form the backbone of community health; their engagement levels serve as vital signs for platform vitality.

Beyond basic metrics, modern power user analysis utilizes sophisticated machine learning techniques to uncover hidden patterns. By applying clustering algorithms like K-means, you can segment users based on multiple engagement indicators, including Lness. This approach reveals natural user groupings and engagement patterns that might otherwise go unnoticed.

The key to effective clustering is finding the sweet spot—typically three to five distinct segments that tell a clear story about your user base. The "elbow method" approach helps to identify the optimal number of segments and ensures enough homogeneousness within a cluster and practical applicability.

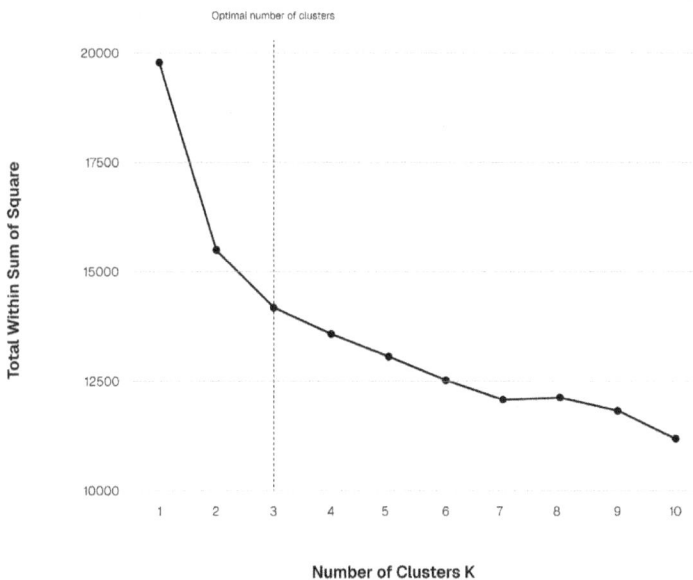

Figure 5-5: Total within sum of squares by number of clusters

To identify power user clusters versus casual user clusters, analyze the statistical patterns within each segment. Compare key engagement metrics like average session duration, feature usage frequency, and interaction depth across clusters. The cluster with consistently higher engagement metrics typically represents your power users. For example, if one cluster shows five times higher daily active minutes and three times more feature interactions than others, that's a strong indicator of power user behavior. While quantitative analysis guides this classification, incorporating qualitative insights from user interviews and behavioral patterns validates and refines your segmentation strategy.

These power users not only drive revenue through increased usage and premium feature adoption, but they also act as valuable product evangelists. They provide authentic word-of-mouth marketing and offer deep insights for product development. Moreover, they often reveal advanced use cases and feature requests that can shape your product road map.

Once you identify your power users, how can you leverage their insights to build a better product? Consider power users as the heartbeat of your product ecosystem. Their journey from identification to full engagement follows a natural progression that builds momentum at each stage:

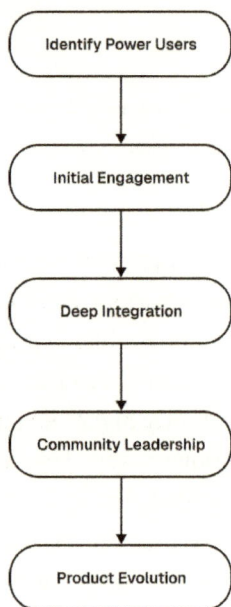

Figure 5-6: Power user impact framework

The story begins with discovery. Identifying power users, like finding rare gems in a mine, reveals individuals whose engagement patterns shine brighter than others. These users naturally gravitate toward deeper product functionality and often uncover creative uses you had not imagined.

As you engage with these power users, prioritize building relationships rather than merely collecting feedback. Start by offering exclusive beta testing opportunities and advisory roles. Invite these users into your product's inner circle, where their insights can shape future development.

The relationship deepens as power users integrate into your product ecosystem. They evolve from simple users into product advocates, sharing their expertise through mentorship programs and community leadership. Their success stories become powerful testimonials, inspiring others.

The final stage is perhaps the most valuable: power users directly influencing product evolution. The image that follows shows how power user analytics could affect the product development cycle. Their usage patterns serve as blueprints for feature development, their workflows inspire onboarding improvements, and their feedback guides strategic priorities. This creates a virtuous cycle where power user engagement drives product improvement, attracting and generating even more power users.

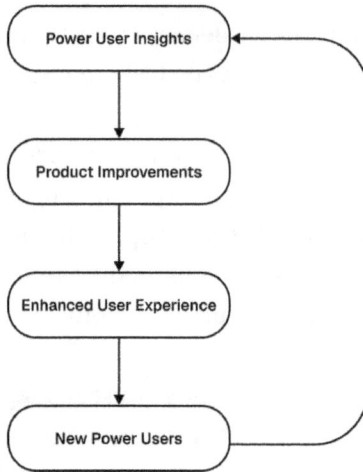

Figure 5-7: The role of power user insights in product development cycle

This cyclical relationship transforms power users from mere statistics into strategic partners in your product's success. Their journey from active users to product champions fosters a sustainable engine for growth and innovation.

TAKEAWAY

Product stickiness—the cornerstone of user engagement—reveals how deeply embedded your product becomes in users' daily lives. We measure this crucial metric through two powerful lenses:

- **DAU/MAU ratio:** This key metric reveals your product's daily magnetic pull, showing the percentage of monthly users who return each day for more.
- **Lness score:** This sophisticated measure captures engagement intensity by tracking active days, offering deep insights into user behavior patterns.

The Lness framework, together with its weekly (Wness) and monthly (Mness) counterparts, provides a comprehensive view of user engagement across various time horizons. These metrics act as your radar system for identifying power users, anticipating churn risks, and developing strategies that convert casual users into devoted advocates.

By combining these engagement metrics with retention analysis and growth accounting, we unlock the trinity of product market fit. Outstanding products excel in all three dimensions: strong user retention, sustainable growth, and compelling stickiness. This powerful combination signals not only product success, but also indicates market dominance.

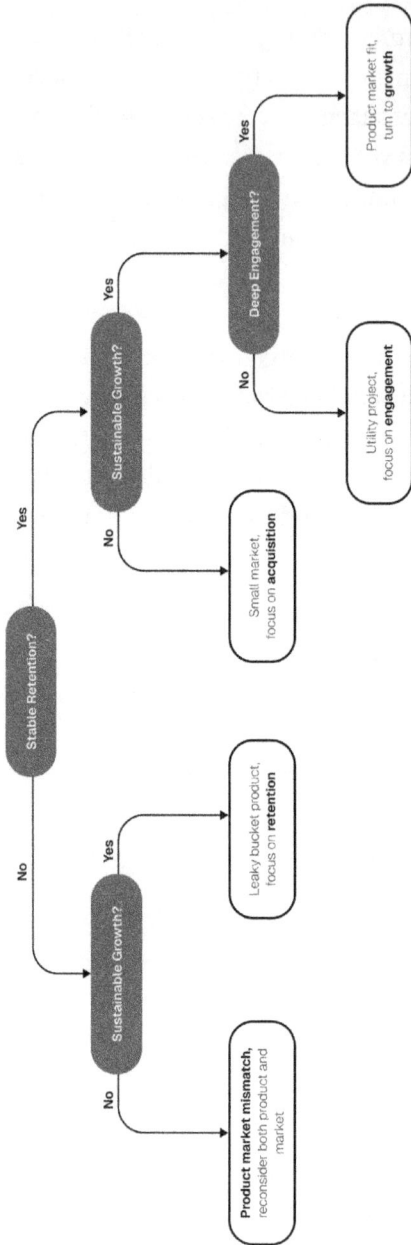

Figure 5-8: The trinity of product market fit

To improve products that underperform in any of these measures before scaling further, refer to the Figure 5-8 PMF playbook for actionable recommendations tailored to each end state. For example, products with high retention but lacking sustainable growth should prioritize acquisition, particularly focusing on the "new" and "resurrected" components of the net growth formula.

EXERCISE

To complete our understanding of this chapter, let's next analyze a real-world product's engagement metrics using the frameworks we've discussed. We'll examine a hypothetical educational app's user data for Q4 2024:

MONTH	MAU	DAU	DAU/MAU	USERS WITH L30 > 20
October	100,000	35,000	0.35	8,500
November	120,000	48,000	0.40	11,000
December	95,000	33,250	0.35	7,600

QUESTIONS

Question 1: Calculate and analyze the power user percentage for each month. What trends do you notice?

Question 2: The DAU/MAU ratio remained relatively stable except for November. What factors might explain the November increase, and what strategies would you recommend to maintain that higher engagement level?

Question 3: December shows a decline across all metrics. Using the concepts from this chapter, design a reengagement strategy targeting:

1. Casual users (L30 < 10)
2. Core users (L30 between 10–20)
3. Power users (L30 > 20)

Question 4: If you were the product manager, what three specific product features would you prioritize to improve the Lness score based on this data?

Bonus Challenge: Create a visualization showing the relationship between user segments and total platform activity, similar to the cumulative Lness graph discussed in the chapter.

ANSWERS

Question 1: Calculate and analyze the power user percentage for each month. What trends do you notice?

Answer: Power user percentages:

1. October: 8.5 percent (8,500/100,000)
2. November: 9.2 percent (11,000/120,000)
3. December: 8.0 percent (7,600/95,000)

Trends:

1. The power user percentage hovers around the typical 10 percent benchmark mentioned in this chapter.

2. November shows the healthiest power user ratio, correlating with the highest DAU/MAU.
3. December's decline might indicate seasonal effects (holidays) or engagement issues requiring attention.

Question 2: The DAU/MAU ratio remained relatively stable except for November. What factors might explain the November increase, and what strategies would you recommend to maintain that higher engagement level?

Answer: Potential factors for November's increase:

1. Seasonal engagement (e.g., exam preparation period)
2. Successful feature launch or promotion
3. Effective reengagement campaign

Recommended strategies:

1. Analyze November's successful engagement tactics and replicate them.
2. Implement achievement-based motivation systems that worked well.
3. Create periodic high-engagement events similar to November's activities.
4. Develop targeted campaigns based on November's user behavior patterns.

Question 3: December shows a decline across all metrics. Using the concepts from this chapter, design a reengagement strategy targeting:

1. Casual users (L30 < 10)

2. Core users (L30 between 10–20)
3. Power users (L30 > 20)

Answer: Reengagement strategies by segment:

1. Casual Users (L30 < 10):
   A. Implement "quick win" achievements.
   B. Offer limited-time comeback bonuses.
   C. Simplify onboarding and core features.
2. Core Users (L30 10–20):
   A. Create midlevel challenges and rewards.
   B. Introduce social features and group activities.
   C. Provide personalized content recommendations.
3. Power Users (L30 > 20):
   A. Launch exclusive beta testing opportunities.
   B. Develop ambassador programs.
   C. Offer advanced features and customization options.
   D. Create leadership opportunities within the community.

Question 4: If you were the product manager, what three specific product features would you prioritize to improve the Lness score based on this data?

Answer: Priority features to improve Lness:

1. Daily Streak System
   A. Gamified daily check-ins
   B. Progressive rewards
   C. Social sharing of achievements
   D. Impact: Increases daily engagement habits
2. Personalized Activity Feed
   A. AI-driven content recommendations

B. Time-sensitive relevant content

C. User behavior-based customization

D. Impact: Makes daily visits more meaningful

3. Community Challenges

A. Weekly/monthly group activities

B. Peer accountability features

C. Progress tracking and leaderboards

D. Impact: Creates social motivation for regular engagement

Bonus Challenge: Create a visualization showing the relationship between user segments and total platform activity, similar to the cumulative Lness graph discussed in the chapter.

Answer:

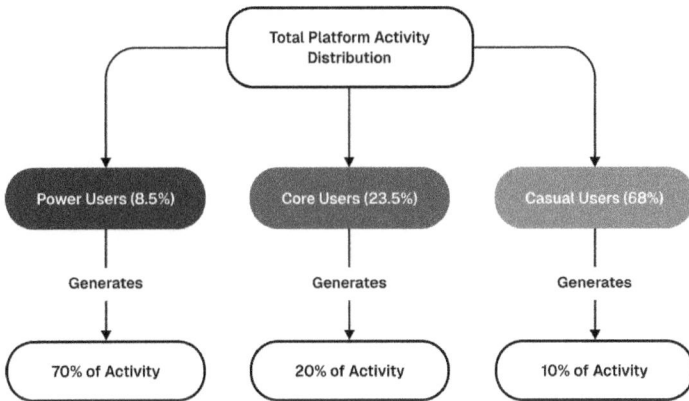

Figure 5-9: User count and activity by segment

This visualization demonstrates the disproportionate impact of power users on total platform activity, confirming the 90/10 principle discussed in this chapter.

Chapter 6

RESURRECT CHURNED CUSTOMERS: STRATEGIES FOR REENGAGEMENT

Picture this: You've built an amazing product that users love. Your retention strategies are effective, engagement is high, and everything seems ideal. But then, it happens—users start to vanish. This phenomenon, known as **churn**, is a silent threat to even the most promising products. The good news is that by understanding why users leave and knowing how to bring them back—through resurrection—you can turn this challenge into an opportunity for sustainable growth.

In this chapter, we'll explore the captivating world of churn analysis and user resurrection and reveal powerful frameworks to predict when users may leave, develop proactive strategies to prevent it, and master the techniques for reengaging those who've drifted away. Think of it as learning to recognize the early warning signs and having a rescue plan in place—essential skills for ensuring long-term success for any product.

CHURN

Some users will inevitably leave your product. This is a natural part of the growth cycle we discussed in Chapter 2. However, not all churn is the same. There are three distinct types:

- **Usage churn:** when users stop engaging with your product
- **Payment churn:** when users discontinue their payments for your product
- **Inorganic churn:** when users leave due to external factors like account deletion or integrity issues

Understanding the different types of churn is crucial for developing targeted retention strategies.

Determining whether a user has truly churned "forever" is like trying to predict the future. Since we cannot wait indefinitely for clarity, we utilize time-bound definitions. Sometimes apparent churn is actually just a reflection of the user's natural usage pattern. For example, if you are viewing a twenty-eight-day window of activity for a quarterly user who only uses your product every three months, they might mistakenly appear to have "churned."

The reasons behind churn are as diverse as your users. Through surveys, we've uncovered common themes that contribute to churn:

- Higher costs drive users away.
- Competitors offer better alternatives.
- The product has not evolved to meet changing user needs.
- Users face frustrating performance issues.
- Users receive inadequate customer support.

While these varied reasons can contribute to user churn, the good news is that by addressing them, you can make improvements to your product. Each reason is a clue that helps teams build better, more sticky features, ultimately enhancing user satisfaction and retention.

The crucial moment to prevent churn occurs just before it happens. In the case of usage churn, while we cannot always predict when a user will leave for good, we can identify red flags such as app crashes or performance issues. Quick, proactive communication about solutions can make a significant difference. Payment churn is more straightforward: when users click the cancel button, you have one last opportunity to engage them. This is the moment to remind them of the value of your premium features and consider offering targeted promotions, like a one-month discount, that might persuade them to stay.

Figure 6-1: Example downgrade model

If users who were once active daily are gradually becoming disengaged, by the time they click the cancel subscription button, it may be too late as they have likely experienced dissatisfaction for weeks. To address this, it is important to closely monitor user behavior to identify signs of disengagement before users decide to leave. This highlights the importance of effective churn analysis.

CHURN ANALYSIS

Just as we consider retention over time—"Are users still with us after seven days? Twenty-eight days? Ninety days?"—churn represents the flip side of the same coin. While retention asks, "Are they still here?" churn asks, "Have they left?" Both questions require a specific time frame to be meaningful.

Let's look at two different ways we measure and understand churn:

- **Growth accounting churn** is a historical metric that looks back and tells us how many users we've already lost. When we say "5 percent of users churned last month," we're using growth accounting to understand our past performance and overall user base health.
- **Churn analysis**, on the other hand, looks forward. Instead of just counting who's already gone, it helps us predict who might leave and why. By analyzing patterns and risk factors, we can identify those at-risk users and adjust our strategy. For example, knowing that users who experience three failed payments are 80 percent likely to leave next month allows you an opportunity to change and improve the payment experience before those users leave.

The challenge lies in determining when to declare a user truly "gone." For some products, it's straightforward: they cancel their subscription, and that's the end. For other products, determining churn is more complex. A daily app user might be considered churned after a week of silence, while a seasonal product might take months before raising any alarms. Just as we measure retention differently based on product type (Daily Active Users vs. Monthly Active Users), the churn windows must align with your product's natural usage patterns.

In successful products, identifying potential churners presents a unique challenge because there are usually very few examples to learn from. It resembles trying to detect a faint signal amid a sea of noise. The key is to create sensitive systems that can recognize subtle signs of dissatisfaction or disengagement before users actually decide to leave.

When addressing the challenge of imbalanced data in churn analysis, you have several powerful tools in your churn analysis toolkit:

- **Resampling techniques:** Use methods like Synthetic Minority Oversampling Technique (SMOTE) to create copies of rare churned data, allowing for better analysis.
- **Class weights:** Assign greater importance to churned user cases, similar to how you would prioritize VIP customers.
- **Alternative metrics:** Employ sophisticated measures like precision and recall, rather than simply counting wins, to gain a deeper understanding of your model's performance.
- **Ensemble methods:** Harness the insights of diverse algorithms like random forest and gradient boosting instead of relying on a single approach.

However, having a strong prediction model is just the start. The real impact occurs when you translate these insights into actionable strategies:

- **Targeted interventions:** Develop personalized experiences for at-risk users, much like a doctor prescribing preventive care.
- **Resource allocation:** Direct your customer success team's efforts toward the users who require the most support.
- **Product improvements:** Analyze data patterns to build better features, like fixing a leaky boat before it sinks.
- **Proactive communication:** Reach out to users at the right time with the right message, just like a friend who anticipates your need for support.
- **Human intervention:** Offer personal touches for your most valuable accounts, recognizing that sometimes, nothing compares to a genuine human connection.

Success in churn analysis lies in acting on these churn predictors before it's too late, turning potential losses into wins through collaborative efforts between data teams and customer-facing staff.

Notifications

New

It's **Jack**'s birthday today. Help him celebrate!

1h

Earlier

TechCrunch shared a new article: 'AI Startup Raises $50M in Series B Funding Round'.

12h

You have a new friend suggestion: **Emma Chen**.

1d

Marcus shared a memory from 2019.

2d

Maya and 12 others liked your post about weekend plans.

1w

Alex commented on your photo.

2w

Check out this **vintage guitar** near you - only $450! Similar to items you've viewed recently

12h

Home   Friends   Marketplace   Feeds   Notifications   Menu

Figure 6-2: Example FB notification tab (Source: Weijun C., Yan Q., Yuwen Z., Christina B., Akos L., Harivardan J., "Notifications: Why Less Is More—How Facebook Has Been Increasing Both User Satisfaction and App Usage by Sending Only a Few Notifications," *Medium*, December 19, 2022, https://medium.com/@AnalyticsAtMeta/notifications-why-less-is-more-how-facebook-has-been-increasing-both-user-satisfaction-and-app-9463f7325e7d.

REAL-WORLD EXAMPLE: THE AI CHAT APP

Let's dive into a real-world scenario: imagine trying to predict which users might leave an AI chat app in the next month. We look at various signals:

- **Usage patterns:** How often do users chat? How long do they stay? What is their rhythm of usage?
- **Engagement metrics:** Are they completing conversations? Do they seem satisfied?
- **Technical indicators:** Are there any frustrating errors or delays they've encountered or reported?
- **User characteristics:** What is their subscription level, loyalty, and history?

In our analysis, we discovered something fascinating: users who hit multiple technical snags in their first week were much more likely to leave. Armed with this key insight, our team implemented automatic error detection and started offering compensation like bonus credits. We also added features to make conversations more engaging and turned potential churners into loyal users.

RESURRECTION

When a user churns, does it mean they're gone forever? In most cases, the answer is no. Users who return to the product after churning are termed "**resurrected**" users.

Why does resurrection work? These users are already familiar with the product and have established a history that may encourage their return, such as the network they've built in a social app. If users have not unsubscribed from emails, you can reach them with exciting offers and new features. A push notification about a friend's activity can spark curiosity and prompt them to return to the app. Additionally, untrackable events may play a role, such as users seeing an ad for your new features on YouTube, leading them to give the app another try.

BRINGING USERS BACK: THE ART OF SMART NOTIFICATIONS

Notifications serve as a powerful tool for user resurrection, but they must be used wisely. Here's how to craft notifications that users genuinely want to receive.

The notification toolkit includes four powerful key components: **push notifications** for immediate engagement, particularly with low-engaged users; **emails** for detailed communications; **SMS** for urgent matters; and **in-app notifications** for active users. For user resurrection, focus on the first three, which are direct lines to dormant users.

In-app notifications function as an internal messaging system—ranging from subtle header banners to eye-catching pop-ups. The goal is to orchestrate these touchpoints into a harmonious flow rather than a disjointed barrage of interruptions.

External notifications—push, email, SMS—require a delicate touch. They're like knocking on someone's door; it's essential to have a compelling reason for interrupting their day.

Three golden rules guide effective notification strategy:

- **Relevance:** Personally craft every notification. "We miss you!" will not cut it—but "Your friend just posted about your favorite topic" might.

- **Frequency:** Find the sweet spot between staying top-of-mind and becoming annoying. Less is often more.
- **Control:** Put users in the driver's seat with granular notification preferences. Trust builds loyalty.

Let's next explore how to master each dimension.

Craft Effective Notifications

First, forget about legally mandated notifications—those operate under different guidelines. For all other notifications, focus on two key metrics: click-through rate (CTR) and conversion rate (CVR). These metrics indicate whether users find your notifications engaging enough to act on.

Leverage machine learning as a valuable tool. By analyzing patterns in user behavior, timing, and content, you can anticipate which notifications will resonate with various user segments. However, do not get too caught up in the data—some of the most impactful notifications, like Facebook's "like" alerts, foster joy without requiring user action.

Find the Perfect Frequency

Be cautious of notification fatigue. Whether you enforce strict daily limits or use dynamic thresholds based on user engagement, your goal should be to add value without overwhelming users.

Research from major tech companies reveals a surprising fact:

at high notification volumes, users develop a tolerance and begin treating notifications like background noise rather than interruptions, achieving "zero inbox" immunity.

Optimize Your Opt-in Strategy

Consider the platform: iOS users can silence notifications more easily than Android users. Smart companies tailor their strategies accordingly and use predictive models to protect their notification privileges. If there is a risk that users might disable notifications, proactively adjust your approach before they reach their tipping point.

Embrace the "Less Is More" Philosophy

You may wonder if sending fewer notifications could negatively impact user engagement. Here's where a compelling paradox emerges. Facebook's Notifications Data Science team revealed that reducing notification volume can actually enhance user satisfaction and app engagement. The team discovered that by implementing a "less is more" approach and focusing on high-quality, relevant notifications, they could achieve better results than with high-volume strategies.

The study also found that users who received fewer, more targeted notifications were more likely to engage meaningfully with the app. This discovery aligns perfectly with our earlier discussion about notification fatigue and the importance of relevance. Facebook's experience demonstrates that sometimes, showing restraint in notification frequency can actually strengthen user engagement and loyalty.

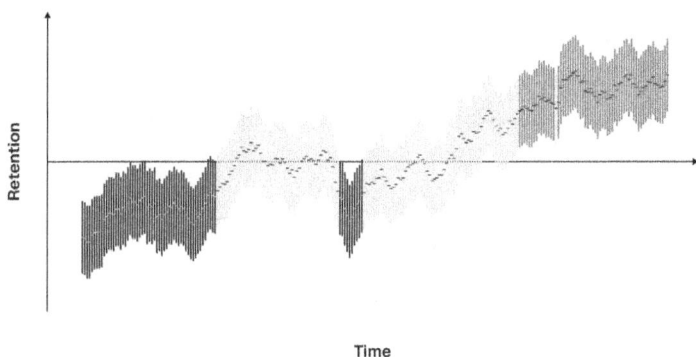

Figure 6-3: Long-term experiment suggests people will eventually return and become even more engaged with Facebook if the change truly improves their experience. (Source: Weijun, "Notifications: Why Less Is More.")

This real-world example reinforces our key principles of notification strategy: prioritizing quality over quantity, respecting user attention, and ensuring each notification delivers genuine value. By applying these lessons, we can build more effective resurrection campaigns that users genuinely appreciate.

THE POWER OF CROSS-APP SYNERGY

For companies with multiple apps, cross-promotion is not just an opportunity—it's a strategic advantage. When users churn from one app but stay active in another, you have a unique chance to reengage them with cross-app promotion because:

- Users already trust your ecosystem.
- Rich user data enables hyper-personalized outreach.
- Reengagement costs less than new user acquisition.

Keys to successful cross-promotion include:

- Perfect timing: Reach users when they're most receptive.

- Clear value: Show exactly how the promoted app enhances their experience.
- Seamless transitions: Make switching between apps effortless.

Aggressive promotion can backfire, which is why it's important to carefully monitor overall engagement. One overzealous campaign can drive users away from your entire ecosystem. Remember, the goal is to enhance, not interrupt, the user experience.

TAKEAWAY

Understanding and managing churn while developing resurrection strategies is essential for sustainable product growth. Here are the key points to consider:

- **Churn analysis is complex:** Analyze churn using specialized techniques like resampling and appropriate metrics to create effective prediction models.
- **Early intervention is critical:** Identify at-risk users with predictive models and implement targeted interventions to prevent churn.
- **Resurrection is possible:** Bring back churned users through strategic notifications and cross-app promotion.
- **Smart notification strategy:** Design notification systems that prioritize relevance, optimal frequency, and user preferences.
- **Cross-app promotion:** Leverage your existing ecosystem effectively and monitor overall engagement to ensure promotions enhance rather than detract from the user experience.

Success in managing churn and resurrection requires a balanced approach between data-driven insights and user-centric strategies. Rather than solely working to prevent users from leaving, aim to create meaningful reengagement that enhances the user's experience with your product.

EXERCISE

Imagine you are a product manager at a meditation app company. Looking at your data, you notice:

- 10,000 Monthly Active Users.
- 7 percent monthly churn rate.
- 2 percent resurrection rate of previously churned users.
- 25 percent of churned users had technical issues in their first week.
- Users who receive more than five notifications per day are three times more likely to churn.

QUESTIONS

Question 1: How many users do you lose to churn each month?

Question 2: If your resurrection rate stays constant, how many users will you bring back next month?

Question 3: Based on the technical issues data, how many churned users might you have retained with better error handling?

Question 4: What would be a good daily notification limit to test, and why?

Bonus Challenge: Design a notification strategy to improve your resurrection rate by 50 percent. Include specific messaging examples and timing considerations.

ANSWERS

Question 1: How many users do you lose to churn each month?

Answer: Monthly churn = 10,000 × 7 percent = 700 users lost per month

Question 2: If your resurrection rate stays constant, how many users will you bring back next month?

Answer: Resurrected users = 700 × 2 percent = 14 users brought back

Question 3: Based on the technical issues data, how many churned users might you have retained with better error handling?

Answer: Preventable churn = 700 × 25 percent = 175 users could have been retained with better technical support

Question 4: What would be a good daily notification limit to test, and why?

Answer: A limit of three to four notifications per day would be reasonable to test, as it's below the risk threshold of five while still allowing important communications.

Bonus Challenge: Design a notification strategy to improve your resurrection rate by 50 percent. Include specific messaging examples and timing considerations.

Answer: Post your answer on LinkedIn and tag the authors for a comment.

Chapter 7

ACCELERATE USER CONVERSION FOR INCREASED REVENUE GENERATION

In today's digital marketplace, mastering revenue generation is essential for product success. Growth data science acts as a compass, guiding this journey by illuminating critical insights into user behavior, conversion patterns, and untapped monetization opportunities. This chapter reveals the powerful intersection of revenue models, growth strategies, and data-driven decision-making that can transform your product's financial trajectory.

In this chapter, we explore successful revenue models, identify the drivers of sustainable growth, and discover how data science can unlock hidden revenue potential for your product.

REVENUE MODELS: A DEEP DIVE
WITH REAL-WORLD EXAMPLES

Consider revenue models as the engines that power your product's growth. Each model offers a unique method for capturing value, similar to different vehicles designed for different terrains. Some products excel with a single engine, while others blend multiple models to create a powerful hybrid that maximizes revenue potential.

Explore strategies like the freemium approach that converts casual users into paying customers, or subscription models that foster lasting relationships. Each strategy presents distinct advantages and challenges. Examine how these models function in practice by drawing insights from some of the most successful companies in the digital landscape. For each revenue model, we'll explore the most important metrics to track—looking at them through two lenses: User Engagement & Conversion Analytics and Revenue Performance Indicators.

1. FREEMIUM MODEL: THE SPOTIFY STORY

The freemium model offers basic features at no cost while reserving premium capabilities for paying users. For example, Spotify allows free users to listen to music with ads, while premium users enjoy features like off-line listening and an ad-free experience.

User Engagement & Conversion Analytics:

1. **Free tier usage metrics:** Monitor Daily Active Users/ Monthly Active Users (DAU/MAU) of free features, fea-

ture engagement rates, and usage frequency. For example, Spotify tracks how many songs users play per session.

2. **Premium feature exposure:** Measure the percentage of users encountering premium features and the interaction rate with premium feature prompts, such as when free Spotify users hit skip limits.

3. **Conversion metrics:** Analyze free-to-paid conversion rate, time to first purchase, and conversion rates by feature.

Revenue Performance Indicators:

1. **Feature-specific revenue:** Assess the revenue generated from each premium feature.

2. **Average revenue per user (ARPU):** Total revenue divided by total users. This crucial metric indicates how effectively the platform monetizes its user base.

2. SUBSCRIPTION MODEL: THE NETFLIX EVOLUTION

The subscription model serves as the backbone for modern Software-as-a-Service (SaaS) businesses, strategically layering features across various pricing tiers. Netflix's transition from DVD rentals to streaming tiers exemplifies this evolution—offering options from basic streaming to premium 4K plans with multiple screens.

Key metrics to analyze in a subscription model include:

User Engagement & Conversion Analytics:

- **Subscription activation metrics:** Measure the trial-to-paid conversion rate, the time to subscribe, and the activation rate by tier.
- **Engagement metrics:** Feature usage by tier, the number of active users per subscription, and session frequency.
- **Retention metrics:**
  - Subscription renewal rate: Track the percentage of subscribers who renew their subscription.
  - Churn rate by tier: Calculate the rate at which customers cancel their subscription.
  - Time to churn: Assess how long customers typically remain subscribed before canceling.
- **Upgrade/downgrade metrics:**
  - Tier transition rates: Analyze how often users switch between subscription tiers.
  - Time to upgrade: Measure the time to upgrade to determine how long users stay at each tier before upgrading.
  - Upgrade retention rate: Understand how long upgraded users stay at higher tiers.
- **Customer lifetime value (CLV):** Calculate the average revenue generated per customer over their entire relationship with the product.

Revenue Performance Indicators

1. MRR/ARR and Growth Accounting

Consider monthly recurring revenue (MRR) and annual recurring revenue (ARR) as essential financial metrics for your business.

For example, Sarah operates a digital art subscription service.

Each month, one hundred artists pay $50 for premium features on her platform, generating $5,000 in MRR. This steady monthly income provides a reliable financial foundation. When Sarah looks at her ARR, she's essentially evaluating her yearly revenue potential—$60,000 ($5,000 × 12 months) of predictable revenue.

The story becomes more dynamic with recent changes. Last month, twenty new artists joined her platform, adding $1,000 to MRR. Additionally, five artists upgraded their plans, contributing another $250. However, three artists canceled their subscriptions, which reduced MRR by $150.

As a result, Sarah's new MRR is $6,100, leading to a projected ARR of $73,200. These figures reveal her business's health and growth potential, serving as vital indicators that show whether her business is thriving or needs improvement.

The underlying themes in user growth accounting and business entity growth accounting are similar in that they:

- Decompose MRR/ARR into distinct statuses.
- Identify the most critical factors driving the net growth of the product. For example, this might be day-over-day or week-over-week growth.

A significant adaptation of the traditional growth accounting framework can be observed in the *retained* bucket. Many SaaS businesses offer various pricing tiers that allow users to move up or down. Although these users are all categorized as "retained," their contributions to ARR can differ significantly. Therefore, account for these transitions as **upgrades**

or downgrades in ARR/MRR. Additionally, some SaaS products bill clients based on the number of seats they use. As the seat count increases, the ARR/MRR grows correspondingly, contributing to the **expansion** ARR/MRR category.

The MRR/ARR decomposition can be represented as:

$$\text{Net MRR} = \text{New MRR} + \text{Reactivated MRR} + \text{Upgraded MRR} + \text{Expansion MRR} - \text{Downgraded MRR} - \text{Churned MRR}$$

An Example of How to Analyze Revenue Trends

Figure 7-1 shows the MRR changes over time from January 2020 to March 2021. The following chart breaks down MRR into different categories:

- **Upgraded MRR:** Represents the revenue from customers upgrading their subscriptions.
- **Reactivated MRR:** Represents the revenue from customers who reactivated their subscriptions from a previously churned state.
- **New MRR:** Represents the revenue from new customers.
- **Downgraded MRR:** Represents the revenue lost from customers downgrading their plans.
- **Churned MRR:** Represents the revenue lost from customers who canceled their subscriptions.

Figure 7-1 indicates that upgraded MRR contributes most significantly to net growth, while downgrades account for the largest revenue decline. This observation suggests that higher-tier offerings may not provide enough value for customers to maintain their upgraded status, likely reflecting that upgrades driven by promotional offers tend to revert to lower tiers in subsequent months.

To gain deeper insights into these patterns, segment the analysis by customer categories and cohorts to identify trends in rapid downgrades. Additionally, the stagnant new ARR highlights the need to optimize top-of-funnel growth and conversion rates.

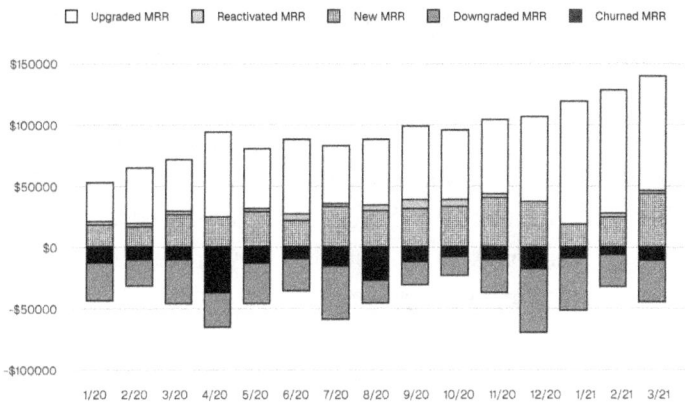

Figure 7-1: MRR breakdown by growth accounting buckets

2. Net Revenue Growth Gross Revenue Growth

Net revenue retention (NRR), also known as net dollar retention (NDR), measures how much recurring revenue you retain from your existing customers over time, including expansions, contractions, and churn. It's calculated as:

$$\text{NRR} = (\text{Starting MRR} + \text{Expansions} - \text{Contractions} - \text{Churn}) \div \text{Starting MRR} \times 100$$

To connect NRR with the MRR concept, consider Sarah's digital art subscription service that was presented earlier in this chapter. Consider how NRR would work in her case. In January, Sarah had one hundred artists paying $50 each ($5,000 MRR). Over the next month:

- Fifteen existing artists upgraded to a $75 plan (+$375).
- Five artists downgraded to a $25 plan (–$125).
- Three artists canceled (–$150).

By February, from those same original customers, Sarah now has $5,100 in revenue. Her NRR is ($5,100 ÷ $5,000) × 100 = 102%.

An NRR above 100 percent signals an important insight for Sarah: despite losing some customers and experiencing downgrades, the revenue growth from upgrades exceeds the losses. Think of it as a bucket with a small leak; you are filling it with more water than you are losing.

This concept directly relates to MRR growth accounting, where tracking upgrades, downgrades, and churn provides a comprehensive view of the overall health of recurring revenue.

The math formula is as follows:

(Current Period Revenue from Existing Customers) ÷
(Previous Period Revenue from Same Customers) × 100

An NRR above 100 percent indicates that revenue growth from existing customers (through expansions) exceeds revenue losses (from downgrades and churn). Most successful SaaS companies aim for an NRR of at least 100 percent.

Gross revenue retention (GRR) measures how well you retain revenue from existing customers, excluding expansions. It only considers downgrades and churn.

To understand GRR, again consider Sarah's digital art subscription service. Sarah started with one hundred artists paying $50 each ($5,000 MRR) in January.

By February, after considering downgrades and churn (but excluding upgrades):

- Five artists downgraded to $25 (–$125).
- Three artists canceled (–$150).

So the GRR calculation is:

- Previous period revenue: $5,000
- Current period revenue (excluding expansions): $4,725 ($5,000 – $125 – $150)

$$GRR = (\$4,725 \div \$5,000) \times 100 = 94.5 \text{ percent}$$

This shows that Sarah retained 94.5 percent of her original revenue when only considering downgrades and churn, ignoring any growth from upgrades.

The math formula of GRR is:

$$(\text{Current Period Revenue from Existing Customers} - \text{Expansion Revenue}) \div (\text{Previous Period Revenue from the Same Customer}) \times 100$$

GRR can never exceed 100 percent as it excludes expansion revenue. A higher GRR indicates better core revenue retention and customer satisfaction. Enterprise SaaS companies typically aim for a GRR of 90 percent or higher.

These metrics are crucial to understanding the health of your recurring revenue and optimizing the effectiveness of your retention and expansion strategies. A high NRR with a solid GRR suggests both strong customer satisfaction and successful upselling/cross-selling efforts.

3. PAY-PER-USE MODEL: THE AMAZON WEB SERVICES CLOUD COMPUTING REVOLUTION

Amazon Web Services (AWS) revolutionized cloud computing with its pay-per-use model. Users only pay for the computing resources they actually use, making it accessible for startups while scaling seamlessly for enterprises.

Track the following key metrics in a pay-per-use model:

User Engagement and Conversion Analytics:

- **Revenue analytics:**
  - **Transaction insights:** Track vital metrics including average purchase value, usage frequency, and revenue per interaction.
  - **Profitability analysis:** Measure unit economics through detailed cost analysis and margin calculations across usage tiers.
  - **Dynamic pricing strategy:** Implement sophisticated price elasticity analysis to optimize revenue.

- User engagement metrics:
  - **Usage milestones:** Identify critical transition points where users reach usage limits.
  - **Purchase behavior:** Analyze temporal patterns in user spending.
  - **Price response:** Monitor usage elasticity across pricing tiers.

4. ADVERTISING MODEL: THE YOUTUBE SUCCESS STORY

YouTube's advertising model demonstrates how free content can generate substantial revenue through strategic ad placement. Users access content for free while creators and the platform monetize through advertising.

User Engagement & Conversion Analytics:

- **Ad performance metrics:**
  - **Ad impressions and views:** The number of times an ad is displayed or viewed
  - **Click-Through Rate (CTR):** The percentage of users who click on ads
  - **Cost Per Click (CPC):** Average cost per ad click
  - **View completion rate:** Percentage of users who watch an entire video ad
- **User engagement metrics:**
  - **Time spent viewing ads:** Duration of ad engagement
  - **Ad interaction rate:** User actions like clicks and skips
  - **User satisfaction:** Feedback on ad relevance and experience
- **Revenue Performance Indicators:**

- Revenue Per Mille (RPM): Revenue per every one thousand ad impressions
- Average Revenue Per User (ARPU) from ads: Average ad revenue per user
- Ad fill rate: Percentage of ad inventory successfully filled

GROWTH MOTION

Once you understand where the revenue comes from, it's important to understand what fuels its growth, often referred to as growth motions. Like revenue models, these are not mutually exclusive. Usually, at the beginning of a growth journey, products may see more growth led by the product itself or the community. As the products become more suited for enterprise use, sales efforts often become the main driver of revenue.

The choice between product-led growth (PLG) and sales-led growth (SLG) typically depends on three key factors:

1. **Product nature:** Whether users can easily self-serve and quickly understand the value proposition, or whether they need guidance during setup.
2. **Customer base:** Whether the target users are tech-savvy enough to onboard themselves.
3. **Pricing model:** PLG works best with *low-cost, scalable pricing models* (e.g., freemium, pay-as-you-go, or tiered subscription) that encourage self-adoption, while SLG suits *high-cost, contract-based pricing* for enterprise deals. Additionally, SLG must consider whether sales volume can justify the labor costs of maintaining a sales team.

PRODUCT-LED GROWTH: WHEN YOUR PRODUCT DOES THE SELLING

Imagine walking into a store where the products are so intuitive and valuable that they sell themselves. That's product-led growth (PLG) in action. Companies like Slack and Dropbox mastered this approach in their early days, letting their products do the heavy lifting of user acquisition and conversion. The secret? A carefully crafted freemium model that gives users just enough features to fall in love with the product, while keeping the most valuable capabilities behind a strategic paywall.

Think of it as a "try before you buy" experience on steroids. Users get to experience the core value proposition firsthand, making the decision to upgrade feel natural rather than forced. But making this work requires a deep understanding of user behavior and careful optimization at every step.

The Science Behind Self-Service Success

To master PLG, become detectives of user behavior. Here's how to solve the mystery:

- **The critical free-to-paid conversion journey**
  - After users reach your payment page, 45 percent abandon it. Why does this happen? Our funnel analysis reveals these crucial moments of truth.
  - Different users have different stories. Enterprise users often convert at rates that differ dramatically from individual users—understanding these patterns is essential.
- **The art of pricing presentation**
  - It's not just about the numbers; it's about the narrative.

When users visit your pricing page, are they perceiving value or merely focusing on cost? Analyzing every interaction ensures the value proposition stands out.

- **Payment friction points**
  - Every failed payment illustrates a friction point. Tracking success rates across payment methods transforms challenges into seamless transactions.
  - Each error message becomes a learning opportunity to streamline the process.
- **The price is right?**
  - Through careful A/B testing, identify the sweet spot between value and cost. A $9.99 monthly plan versus a $12.99 plan conveys very different messages.
  - Measure how various discount strategies influence user psychology and conversion rates.
- **Mapping the path to purchase**
  - Every successful conversion narrates a story, whether it originates at a feature paywall (30 percent) or the pricing page (25 percent).
  - By identifying these advantageous paths, guide more users toward their aha moment.

SALES-LED GROWTH: THE POWER OF PERSONAL TOUCH

While PLG lets the product do the talking, SLG brings the human element to the forefront. SLG enables skilled sales teams to become trusted advisers, particularly for larger companies where the stakes and potential rewards are higher. SLG prioritizes building relationships, understanding complex needs, and crafting solutions that fit.

Let's dive into the metrics that matter:

- **The Pipeline: Your Revenue Engine**
  - **Pipeline velocity:** Like a well-oiled machine, we track how smoothly deals move through each stage, measuring average time spent in each sales phase and identifying potential bottlenecks.
  - **Win rate analysis:** Learn from victory and setback to refine your approach, with detailed analysis of success factors and areas for improvement.
  - **Deal size patterns:** Understanding where the biggest opportunities lie helps focus our efforts, including historical trends and seasonal variations in deal sizes.
- **Sales Excellence Metrics**
  - **Revenue champions:** Track and learn from our top performers, analyzing their successful strategies and replicating best practices across the team.
  - **Time to close:** Optimize every step of the journey, from first contact to contract signing.
  - **Investment vs. return:** Carefully monitoring CAC ensures sustainable growth, with detailed ROI analysis by customer segment.
  - **Sales activity metrics:** Track key activities like calls made, meetings scheduled, and proposals sent to optimize sales productivity.
- **Growing Customer Value**
  - **Expansion opportunities:** Identify when customers are ready for more through usage patterns and engagement signals.
  - **Cross-sell success:** Find natural fits for complementary solutions based on customer behavior and needs analysis.

- **Health indicators:** Utilize predictive metrics that signal growth potential, including product adoption rates and satisfaction scores.
- **Customer life cycle analysis:** Understand the optimal timing for upsell and expansion conversations.
- **Market Intelligence**
  - **Geographic insights:** Understand regional success patterns and tailor approaches to local market conditions.
  - **Industry champions:** Identify and reinforce commitment on high-performing sectors with detailed vertical analysis.
  - **Market share growth:** Track your expanding footprint through competitive analysis and market penetration metrics.
  - **Economic impact analysis:** Monitor how market conditions affect sales cycles and close rates.

PLG and SLG are not mutually exclusive—in a PLS (product-led sales) motion, PLG-generated leads are passed to sales early based on account activity that signals potential for a large deal, as well as firmographic indicators (e.g., a user from a one hundred-plus employee company).

SPECIAL TOPIC: PRICING AND PACKAGING ANALYSIS

Regardless of whether your product follows PLG or SLG strategies, every data scientist focused on monetization will encounter the challenge of pricing and packaging (P&P) changes. Here's a story illustrating the importance of these changes and how to manage them effectively.

Imagine you are running a successful SaaS product. Over time, adjusting your pricing strategy becomes necessary for several reasons:

- **Market dynamics:** Your main competitor just lowered their prices, and you need to respond.
- **Cost changes:** Your cloud computing costs have increased by 30 percent this year.
- **Value evolution:** You've just launched an amazing AI feature that users love.
- **Customer feedback:** Enterprise customers are asking for more flexibility in your pricing tiers.
- **Business model optimization:** Your board wants to increase profit margins while keeping customers happy.
- **Market expansion:** You are entering the European market and need localized pricing.

THE ART AND SCIENCE OF PRICING

Use data analysis to study user behavior, measure feature adoption, and track conversion metrics. Simultaneously, understand the human elements—users' perception of value, the motivations for their decisions, and the emotional influences on purchasing. When these aspects align, you can create pricing tiers and feature combinations that resonate deeply with users, combining data science with user experience research (UXR) for effective pricing strategies.

- **The pricing journey:** Implement pricing changes with both scientific precision and artistic finesse. Use data analysis to analyze revenue impact and user segments, while also crafting presentations of changes that maintain customer trust. Instead of implementing a blanket price increase, consider developing varied package sizes or designing targeted promotional campaigns based on data insights.

- **Understand user psychology:** Apply data analysis to identify which features receive the most engagement and use this knowledge to determine their importance to users. This understanding allows you to bundle features in ways that naturally encourage upgrades.

- **Measure success:** After launching pricing changes, utilize scientific methods to track their impact. Some changes, like price increases, may yield immediate results; others, like extending trial periods, might take time to demonstrate their impact. Interpreting these results within the broader context of user satisfaction and market dynamics will provide a comprehensive understanding of success.

TAKEAWAY

This chapter highlights several key aspects of revenue generation and growth strategies:

- **Multiple revenue models:** Implement various revenue models including freemium, subscription-based, and advertising-based approaches. Clearly define specific metrics to track and optimize performance in each model to maximize revenue potential.

- **Growth motion strategies:** Understand the distinction between product-led growth (PLG) and sales-led growth (SLG), and choose the appropriate strategy based on product nature, customer base, and pricing model.

- **Data-informed decision-making:** Leverage analytics for funnel optimization, pricing decisions, and user behavior analysis. This approach is vital for driving revenue growth.

- **Pricing and packaging:** Make strategic pricing decisions that balance market dynamics, cost changes, value evolution, and customer needs while maintaining profitability.

To succeed in revenue generation, continuously monitor, analyze, and optimize these elements and remain responsive to market changes and customer needs.

EXERCISE

GROWTH ACCOUNTING STATUS ANALYSIS

Given an SaaS product's MRR data:

January MRR: $100,000

1. New: $20,000 (revenue from new customers who joined in February)
2. Upgraded: $15,000 (additional revenue from existing customers who upgraded in February)
3. Downgraded: –$5,000 (revenue lost from customers who downgraded in February)
4. Churned: –$10,000 (revenue lost from customers who canceled in February)
5. Reactivated: $8,000 (revenue from former customers who returned in February)

QUESTIONS

Question 1: Calculate the total MRR for February.

Question 2: What is the net MRR growth?

Question 3: Which growth accounting state contributed most positively to growth?

Question 4: What strategic recommendations would you make based on this data?

For each exercise, provide detailed solutions and explanations that tie back to the growth accounting principles discussed in this chapter.

ANSWERS

Question 1: Calculate the total MRR for February.

Answer:

$$\text{February MRR} = \text{January MRR} + \text{New} + \text{Upgraded} + \text{Reactivated} - \text{Downgraded} - \text{Churned}$$

$$\text{February MRR} = \$100{,}000 + \$20{,}000 + \$15{,}000 + \$8{,}000 - \$5{,}000 - \$10{,}000 = \$128{,}000$$

Question 2: What is the net MRR growth?

Answer:

$$\text{Net MRR Growth} = \text{February MRR} - \text{January MRR}$$

$$\text{Net MRR Growth} = \$128{,}000 - \$100{,}000 = \$28{,}000$$

$$\text{Net MRR Growth Rate} = (\$28{,}000 \div \$100{,}000) \times 100\% = 28\%$$

Question 3: Which growth accounting state contributed most positively to growth?

Answer: Looking at the positive contributions:

- New MRR: $20,000
- Upgraded MRR: $15,000
- Reactivated MRR: $8,000

The New MRR at $20,000 contributed most positively to growth.

Question 4: What strategic recommendations would you make based on this data?

Answer: Based on this data, I recommend the following priorities:

- **Priority 1: Continue customer acquisition efforts:** Since new customers contribute the most to growth ($20,000), focus resources on maintaining and optimizing successful acquisition channels.
- **Priority 2: Expand upselling initiatives:** With upgrades generating $15,000, there's clear evidence customers value premium offerings. Develop additional upgrade paths to capitalize on this willingness to spend more.
- **Priority 3: Address churn:** The $10,000 lost to churn represents a significant leak in your revenue bucket. Implement targeted retention strategies focusing specifically on customer segments showing the highest churn risk.
- **Secondary focus: Minimize downgrades and leverage reactivations:** While important, addressing the $5,000 in

downgrades and expanding on the $8,000 in reactivations should receive attention after the top three priorities are addressed.

For each exercise, provide detailed solutions and explanations that tie back to the growth accounting principles discussed in this chapter.

Chapter 8

OPTIMIZE PERFORMANCE AND BUILD SUSTAINABLE GROWTH FLYWHEELS

In previous chapters, the fundamental aspects of growth analytics were explored, from understanding user behavior and measuring engagement to conducting experiments and analyzing their results. The discussion included frameworks for identifying opportunities, establishing reliable metrics, and making data-informed decisions to drive product growth.

Now, as the focus shifts to more specialized topics, we'll highlight niche yet crucial topics that experienced growth analysts encounter as their products mature. These advanced concepts build upon our earlier foundations but concentrate on specific levers and mechanisms that can significantly impact product success, particularly when basic growth frameworks are already established.

THE HIDDEN POWER OF PERFORMANCE

Imagine clicking a button and waiting...and waiting...and waiting. Many users have experienced this frustration. Performance—the speed at which a product responds to user actions—can make or break the user experience. Whether it's the initial app launch, a page refresh, or something as simple as typing, every millisecond counts in keeping users engaged and satisfied.

"Performance" and "reliability" are often mistakenly treated as interchangeable terms, but they represent fundamentally different concepts. Think of performance as how fast a car drives, while reliability refers to whether the car starts at all. Reliability focuses on whether the product functions as intended—does it crash? Does it respond? In contrast, performance emphasizes the speed of that response.

When measuring performance through metrics like "Time to do X," the focus shifts from the median user experience to the P90 or P95—the slowest 10 percent or 5 percent of experiences. Why emphasize these extremes? While most users may be satisfied, those experiencing slowdowns are most likely to abandon the product. Improving these extreme cases not only retains at-risk users but often improves the overall experience for everyone.

Consider the typical web page loading time distribution shown in Figure 8-1. Notice how the loading time distribution is skewed to the right—this pattern reveals an important aspect of user experience:

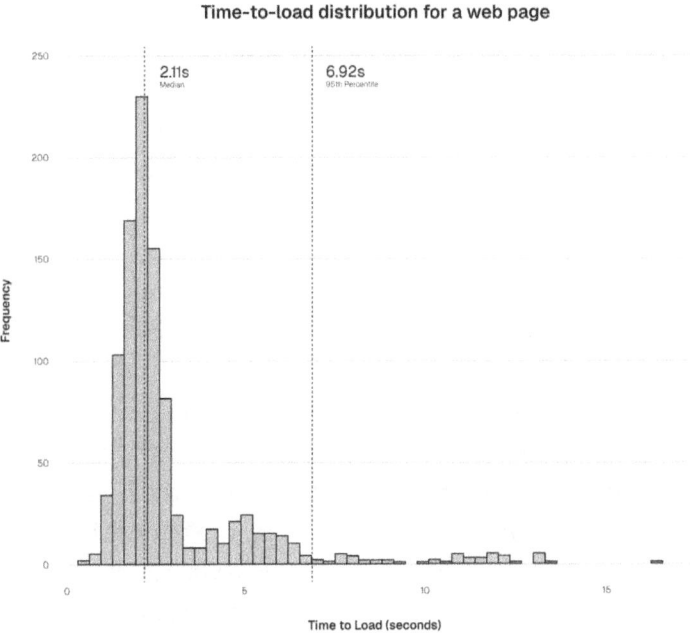

Figure 8-1: Typical web page loading time distribution

Imagine you are a startup founder racing against the clock to launch your product. Performance optimization may seem like a luxury that you cannot afford right now. You need a product that functions well and resonates with users. This scenario is common in the tech industry: performance often takes a backseat during early stages. However, once your product gains traction, that same performance can become a powerful driver of growth.

How can you advocate for investing in performance? Let's explore some compelling data-informed approaches:

- **Exploration analysis:** Approach exploration as detective work. Dive into user logs to uncover the relationship between speed and success. Like a crime scene investigation, piece together evidence by performing logistic regressions on user retention against performance, controlling for variables such as app type, country, and network speed.
  - Map performance patterns across various app types, countries, and workspace sizes to identify your digital fingerprints.
  - Perform rigorous statistical analyses to reveal connections between speed and user retention.
- **Counter experimentation:** Sometimes the best way to showcase the value of performance is to remove it temporarily. Employ A/B/n testing, where you simultaneously test different levels of artificial slowdown. Introduce controlled performance degradation to measure user response. For example, assess how users react to 100ms, 300ms, and 500ms delays. This experimentation reveals the impact of speed on user satisfaction, much like determining how much people value their morning coffee by making them wait an extra minute each day.

Here's the crucial part: not all slowness impacts users equally. Users may patiently wait for a large template to duplicate, but they will quickly lose patience with a sluggish page load. It's all about managing expectations.

To maximize impact, prioritize efforts where they matter most:

- **Top actions:** Focus on essential features that users rely on daily, like document editing. Consider both user engagement and frequency of use.
- **Top surfaces:** Treat these as your storefront—marketing sites, notifications, and navigation. First impressions are critical!
- **Top timing scenarios:** Recognize that different contexts require different speeds. For instance, solo editing and collaborative work demand distinct approaches.

Success hinges on collaboration between data analysts and engineers. Analysts uncover the patterns, while engineers ensure the right metrics are measured—focusing on actual user experience rather than backend processing time.

The final piece of the puzzle involves setting clear targets. By plotting an "abandonment line" that shows how user retention declines with slower performance, you can identify critical thresholds across various regions and devices.

Data reveals a compelling story: user abandonment begins as a trickle, escalates into a flood after three to five seconds (the critical threshold), and ultimately stabilizes around 90 percent. Keep these two key figures in mind: the three-*second critical point* where user drop-offs begin, and the *50 percent abandonment rate*, marking the point of no return.

Simulated abandonment rate vs. time-to-load

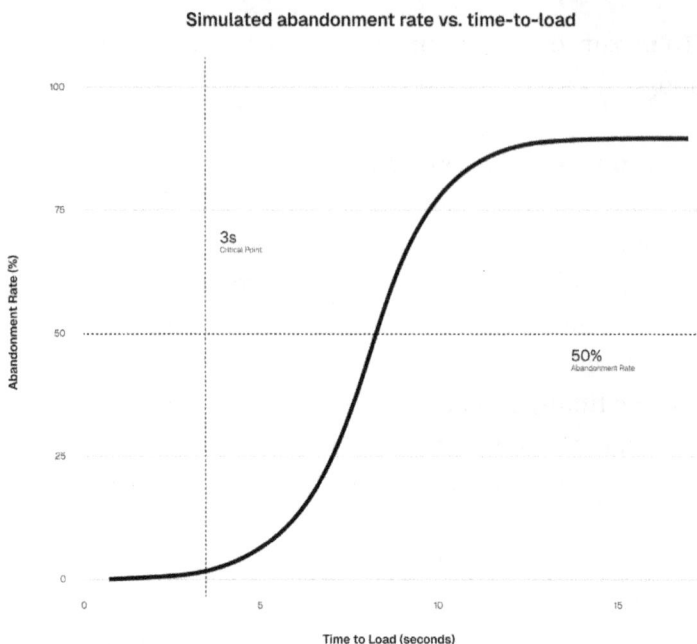

Figure 8-2: Relationship between time-to-load and abandonment rate

Apply this knowledge through A/B testing. Once you've optimized your app's loading time, how can you demonstrate its impact? While the standard A/B testing playbook (see Chapter 10 for details) provides a solid foundation, performance metrics introduce unique considerations. When analyzing percentiles like P90/P95, traditional t-tests may fall short. Measuring the height of the tallest person in a room illustrates this point: average height does not capture the full picture. For these instances, you need specialized statistical tools.

Several companies, including Wish, have pioneered innovative approaches to percentile-based A/B testing. Explore these strategies in an article by Qike Li published on *Medium*: How Wish A/B Tests Percentiles.[3]

THE FLYWHEEL EFFECT: TURNING SMALL WINS INTO UNSTOPPABLE MOMENTUM

Imagine pushing a massive wheel. Initially, it barely moves; each push demands significant effort. However, as you continue, something remarkable happens. The wheel starts to turn more easily, gaining speed with every rotation. This is the essence of a flywheel—a mechanical wonder that converts intermittent energy into steady, consistent power.

In the business realm, Jim Collins highlights this powerful concept in his groundbreaking book *Good to Great.* Just as a physical flywheel changes irregular pushes into smooth motion, a business flywheel transforms small, consistent actions into unstoppable momentum. Each customer success story, product improvement, and positive interaction contributes to this momentum, making future growth increasingly effortless.

Consider the following:

- **Mechanical flywheel:** Nature's momentum machine, storing and smoothing energy like a patient guardian.
- **Business flywheel:** Your growth engine, where today's small wins propel tomorrow's rapid success.

---

3   Qike (Max) Li, "How Wish A/B Tests Percentiles," *Medium*, August 9, 2021, https://medium.com/data-science/how-wish-a-b-tests-percentiles-35ee3e4589e7.

For data scientists, the flywheel serves as more than a metaphor; it's a powerful framework for measuring and driving sustainable growth. Your objective is to collaborate with product teams to identify, measure, and optimize your unique flywheel.

Every product has its own flywheel narrative. In marketplaces, it involves the dynamic interaction between buyers and sellers, each enhancing the platform's value for the other. For content platforms, it reflects the virtuous cycle of creators and consumers—great content attracts more engaged users, inspiring creators to produce even more. Next, we'll explore a real-world example of how this dynamic unfolds:

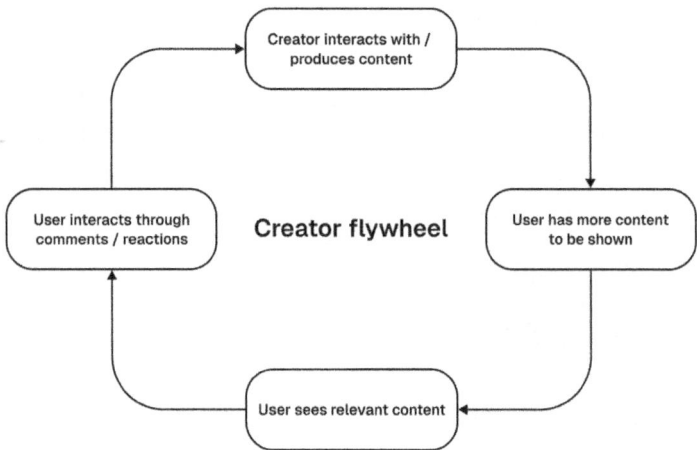

Figure 8-3: The growth flywheel

Imagine a powerful engine of growth that drives both content creation and creator engagement. This is the creator flywheel—a self-reinforcing cycle that transforms individual actions into sustained momentum. Here's how it operates: A creator shares unique content, enriching the platform's content library. Sophisticated ranking algorithms then deliver this content to the ideal audience through personalized feeds. When users discover resonant content, they engage through comments and reactions, creating a vibrant community dialogue. These meaningful interactions motivate creators to engage and connect with their audience to produce even more compelling content, completing and reinforcing the cycle. Like a finely tuned machine, each component amplifies the others, creating an unstoppable force for growth.

To fully harness the true potential of this flywheel, monitor its vital signs regularly. Data scientists play a crucial role in defining and tracking these metrics. For the creator flywheel, consider these key performance indicators to assess whether momentum is building:

1. **Content creation:** Track the number and frequency of posts per creator to measure the lifeblood of your platform.
2. **Content inventory:** Assess the diversity and depth of your content ecosystem by measuring the pool of high-quality, relevant content available to users.
3. **Impressions:** Measure content reach and distribution effectiveness through view counts and engagement rates.
4. **Feedback:** Evaluate community vitality by quantifying user interactions, from quick reactions to thoughtful comments.
5. **Creator interaction:** Gauge community health by analyzing creator responsiveness and engagement with their audience.

By closely monitoring these metrics, you can identify early

warning signs, celebrate successes, and make data-driven decisions to keep the flywheel spinning at optimal speed. Consider this your growth dashboard, where each metric serves as a crucial indicator of your platform's momentum and potential.

BUILDING YOUR GROWTH FLYWHEEL: A STRATEGIC FRAMEWORK

Creating a powerful flywheel involves more than just drawing circles and arrows; it requires orchestrating a self-reinforcing system that drives sustainable growth. Here's your comprehensive guide to building and measuring an effective flywheel:

1. ARCHITECT YOUR FLYWHEEL FOUNDATION

- **Define your growth DNA** by pinpointing the core elements that drive your product's success, including user acquisition and engagement loops.
- **Establish connections** between these elements to clarify the cause-and-effect relationships. For instance, examine how increased user engagement leads to greater word-of-mouth growth.

2. STRUCTURE YOUR GROWTH ENGINE

- Divide your flywheel into clear, actionable stages that form a continuous cycle. Visualize it as a perpetual motion machine where each component enhances the next.
- Ensure each stage generates natural momentum that propels the next stage forward like a perfectly choreographed dance.

3. MEASURE WHAT MATTERS

- For each stage, establish meaningful metrics that accurately reflect performance. Focus on these key areas:
  - **Content creation:** Assess both the quality and quantity of new content.
  - **Content distribution:** Evaluate reach and engagement metrics.
  - **User interaction:** Analyze the depth and frequency of engagement.
  - **Community growth:** Measure network effects and viral coefficients.
  - **Creator success:** Track retention and satisfaction metrics.

4. MONITOR YOUR MOMENTUM

- Implement robust tracking systems to capture the real-time pulse of your flywheel.
- Utilize time-series analysis to identify patterns, predict trends, and detect early warning signs.
- Establish smart performance thresholds that trigger alerts to address small issues before they escalate into major roadblocks.

5. ACCELERATE THROUGH OPTIMIZATION

- Launch targeted experiments to enhance each stage. For example, experiment with different content recommendation algorithms to increase engagement.
- Identify and remove friction points that impede your flywheel's momentum.

6. ALIGN WITH STRATEGIC GOALS

- Ensure that your flywheel directly supports your company's North Star metrics and business objectives.
- Create transparent reporting that clearly illustrates the flywheel's impact on business success.

7. EVOLUTION AND ADAPTATION

- Regularly reassess and refine your flywheel as your product and market conditions evolve.
- Keep your measurement systems agile, ready to adapt to new opportunities as they emerge.

8. POWER THROUGH AUTOMATION

- Develop a robust data infrastructure that automatically collects and visualizes key metrics.
- Implement smart monitoring systems that enable proactive management of potential issues.

A truly effective flywheel relies on data and continuous optimization, not on hope and assumptions. As you implement these strategies, maintain a relentless focus on measuring impact and iterating based on actual results. Your flywheel should be more than just a pretty diagram; it must function as a dynamic growth engine that strengthens with every rotation.

TAKEAWAY

This chapter examines specialized growth analytics topics with a focus on performance metrics and flywheels. Key takeaways include:

- **Performance analysis:** Prioritize P90/P95 metrics over averages and collaborate with engineering to ensure accurate time logging. Utilize abandonment curves to establish meaningful performance targets.
- **Flywheel framework:** Recognize that understanding and implementing flywheels is essential for sustainable growth. Identify, measure, and optimize the unique flywheel of each product.
- **Data-informed approach:** Achieving success in performance optimization and flywheel implementation necessitates:
  - Regular monitoring of key metrics
  - Continuous experimentation and optimization
  - Clear alignment with business objectives
  - Adaptation based on product evolution

When these concepts are effectively implemented, they can significantly enhance your product's growth trajectory and user engagement.

EXERCISE

Let's put your understanding to the test with a real-world scenario. You are a growth analyst at a video streaming platform, and you've noticed some concerning trends in user engagement.

PART 1: PERFORMANCE ANALYSIS

You have the following data about video loading times and user retention:

```
loading_times = {
'P50': 2.1, # seconds
'P90': 4.8,
'P95': 6.2
}
retention_by_loading_time = {
'0-2s': 85%,
'2-4s': 72%,
'4-6s': 45%,
'6-8s': 28%,
'8+s': 12%
}
```

Questions

Question 1: Why should you focus on P90/P95 metrics rather than the median (P50) in this case?

Question 2: Based on the retention data, what would you set as your critical threshold for loading time?

Question 3: Calculate the potential impact on overall retention if you could improve all P90 experiences to load within four seconds.

Answers

Question 1: Why should you focus on P90/P95 metrics rather than the median (P50) in this case?

Answer: P90/P95 metrics capture the worst user experiences, which have a disproportionate impact on retention. While P50 shows the typical experience, poor performance outliers are often what drive users away.

Question 2: Based on the retention data, what would you set as your critical threshold for loading time?

Answer: The critical threshold should be set at four seconds because:

1. There's a dramatic drop in retention from 72 percent to 45 percent after four seconds.
2. This aligns with the industry standard three-to-five-second threshold.
3. It represents a realistic technical goal.

Question 3: Calculate the potential impact on overall retention if you could improve all P90 experiences to load within four seconds.

Answer: Impact calculation:

1. Current P90 at 4.8 seconds falls in the four-to-six second bracket (45 percent retention).
2. Moving to less than four seconds bracket (72 percent retention).
3. Potential improvement: 27 percent higher retention for the slowest 10 percent of experiences.
4. Overall impact: ~2.7 percent increase in total user retention.

PART 2: FLYWHEEL ANALYSIS

Your platform has the following monthly metrics:

```
creator_metrics = {
'active_creators': 1000,
'new_videos_per_creator': 3.2,
'avg_views_per_video': 5000,
'comment_rate': '2.1%', # comments per view
'creator_response_rate': '15%' # % of comments getting
creator responses
}
```

Questions

Question 1: Map out the key components of this platform's creator flywheel.

Question 2: Identify the weakest link in the current flywheel based on the metrics provided.

Question 3: Propose one specific experiment to strengthen this weak point, including your hypothesis and how you would measure success.

Answers

Question 1: Map out the key components of this platform's creator flywheel.

Answer: Key flywheel components:

- Content Creation → Content Inventory
- Content Distribution (views)
- User Engagement (comments)
- Creator Response
- Creator Motivation
- Back to Creation

Question 2: Identify the weakest link in the current flywheel based on the metrics provided.

Answer: Weakest link: Creator response rate at 15 percent is quite low, potentially breaking the engagement loop. This could demotivate users from commenting and reduce creator insights about their audience.

Question 3: Propose one specific experiment to strengthen this weak point, including your hypothesis and how you would measure success.

Answer: Proposed experiment: The hypothesis is that highlighting high-engagement creators (greater than 30 percent response rate) in recommendations will increase overall creator response rates. This is measured by:

- Primary metric: Creator response rate
- Secondary metrics:
  ○ Comment rates
  ○ Creator posting frequency
  ○ View retention success criteria: 25 percent increase in creator response rate over four weeks with no negative impact on secondary metrics.

Chapter 9

SIZE GROWTH OPPORTUNITY AND SET ACHIEVABLE GROWTH GOALS

In the previous chapters, various metrics for measuring product success and team performance were explored. These metrics serve as indicators of progress and growth across different dimensions of the product. Now, a critical question emerges: How can teams be effectively motivated to improve these metrics, and what constitutes a reasonable growth target based on resource investments? This chapter delves deeply into the art and science of goal setting, examining how to establish meaningful targets that are both ambitious and achievable.

Difference between Target and Actual

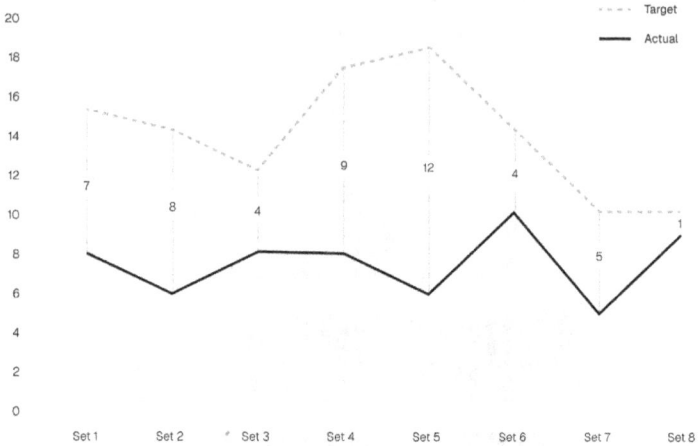

Figure 9-1: A chart illustrating goal achievement, highlighting the difference between actual and target performance.

WHY ARE GOALS NECESSARY?

Goals are essential because they act as a compass, guiding teams toward meaningful impact while providing clarity and purpose. By establishing clear, well-defined goals, teams can unlock their full potential in three critical ways:

1. Focus intently on core user needs, enabling the creation of elegant, effective solutions that deliver maximum value with minimum complexity.
2. Create a consistent link between daily decisions and long-term vision, ensuring that every effort contributes to sustainable, meaningful progress.
3. Navigate complex decisions confidently by balancing key priorities, including growth, quality maintenance, and responsible development practices.

TERMINOLOGY

1. **Goal:** A specific, measurable outcome aimed to be achieved within a defined time frame
2. **Goal metric:** A specific, quantifiable measure used to track progress toward achieving a goal
3. **Counter metric:** A measurement used to balance or counterbalance the primary goal metric, providing a more holistic view of performance
4. **Guardrail metric:** A measurement that ensures progress toward a goal does not lead to undesirable outcomes or compromise other important aspects of the business or product

WHAT TYPES OF GOALS ARE AVAILABLE?

Goals can take different formats depending on the use case. Let's break it down.

GOAL HIERARCHY: FROM TEAM TO COMPANY VISION

Before defining specific team goals, begin with a clear company vision. This overarching vision acts as the North Star, guiding all organizational decisions and objectives.

A well-crafted company vision should be ambitious yet achievable, inspiring but concrete. It should answer fundamental questions like:

- What impact does the company aim to make in the world?
- What transformation should be brought to the industry?
- How can customer service be enhanced or transformed?

Once the company vision is established, it becomes easier to create alignment across different organizational levels, ensuring that team-specific goals meaningfully contribute to the broader company mission.

> 💡 Company-level North Star metrics often lag behind current initiatives and may not directly align with every team's daily activities.

At the team level, goals become more concrete and actionable, directly connecting to daily work while aligning with the company's broader vision. Here's a compelling example that shows how this concept works in practice:

Imagine a data science team working on revolutionizing the shopping experience at a major e-commerce company. Their immediate focus is to create a smarter product recommendation system. Although this might sound like a purely technical endeavor, it generates a powerful ripple effect throughout the organization.

The story unfolds across three levels:

- **Team level:** Data scientists concentrate on making recommendations truly relevant for each customer. They track their success using three key metrics:
  - A target click-through rate of 15 percent, indicating that recommendations capture customers' attention.
  - An average order value of $75, showing that customers discover higher-value items they love.
  - A customer satisfaction score of 4.5/5, confirming that

the recommendations genuinely enhance the shopping experience.

- **Organization level:** These improvements cascade upward, transforming the overall shopping experience:
  - A conversion rate of 3.5 percent as more browsers become buyers.
  - Customers explore an average of five pages per session, reflecting deeper engagement.
  - 40 percent of visitors return, indicating a compelling experience that draws users back.
- **Company level:** Ultimately, these efforts contribute to the company's ambitious growth targets:
  - 20 percent year-over-year revenue growth.
  - 25 percent growth in Monthly Active Users.
  - An impressive net promoter score (NPS) of 65, demonstrating strong customer advocacy.

GOAL CATEGORIES BY PRODUCT NATURE

Product goals manifest in various forms, each serving a distinct role in driving success. These goals, from measuring user engagement to ensuring technical reliability, work together like pieces of a puzzle. Let's explore how different types of goals combine to create a comprehensive view of product performance and guide teams toward significant impact.

1. Usage Goals: The Growth Journey

Envision a product's journey as akin to raising a child. It begins with foundational steps, evolves into a phase of rapid growth, and ultimately matures into its full potential:

A. **Product market fit stage:** Here, we monitor key indicators of user affection—assessing daily active usage and the frequency of return visits, like parents observing their child's first steps.

B. **Growth stage:** In this phase, the product expands its reach. We track new user acquisition and measure how deeply users embrace innovative features, much like watching a teenager explore new interests.

C. **Maturity stage:** At this point, the product integrates into a broader ecosystem, fostering valuable connections and partnerships, like an adult nurturing meaningful relationships.

2. Integrity Goals: Trust as Foundation

Building and maintaining trust is like building your reputation: it requires time to build and can be lost in an instant. In today's digital landscape, safeguarding this trust involves:

A. **Maintaining a spam-free environment:** Like keeping a clean and welcoming home, a spam-free space fosters user confidence.

B. **Ensuring effective user verification:** Like checking IDs at a high-security event, rigorous user verification ensures a trustworthy platform.

C. **Enhancing content quality:** Comparable to a curator carefully choosing pieces for an art gallery, commitment to high-quality content improves user trust and engagement.

3. Reliability Goals: The Technical Foundation

A. **Usability:** Ensure consistent system responsiveness, seamless user interactions, and intuitive navigation across all features and interfaces.

B. **Performance:** Maintain optimal system speed, resource utilization, and response times under varying load conditions to deliver a smooth user experience.

C. **Quality:** Implement robust error handling, conduct regular system health checks, and proactively address technical issues before they impact users.

4. Launch Goals: Shipping Value

Launch goals aim to deliver specific features or capabilities by designated target dates. Although these milestones are not quantitative, they drive innovation and effectively meet market demands. For example, successfully launching a new mobile app by Q3 or releasing a major platform update before the holiday season can generate considerable business value and enhance user experience.

5. Revenue Goals: The Business Impact

Just as a flourishing garden requires both water and sunlight, a successful product depends on financial growth and user trust. Track essential metrics like revenue, average revenue per user, and customer lifetime value while ensuring that product integrity and reliability are never compromised for financial gains.

GOAL TIME FRAME: SETTING THE RIGHT DURATION

Team-level goals generally span medium to long-term horizons, with most organizations setting targets on a quarterly, semiannual, or annual basis. This time frame enables meaningful progress while allowing flexibility to adapt to changing market conditions.

GOAL FORMAT: CHOOSE THE ONE THAT IS MOST MEASURABLE

Setting goals is like choosing between two powerful tools: a telescope and a microscope. Absolute goals, like total paid customers, function like a telescope by providing a broad view and tracking overall progress. In contrast, ratio goals, like free-to-paid conversion rates, act as a microscope, allowing for a detailed examination of your product's performance.

When should you use each tool? Utilize your telescope (absolute goals) for company-wide navigation and long-term planning. Employ your microscope (ratio goals) when conducting experiments and analyzing precise cause-and-effect relationships.

For the most comprehensive perspective, use these tools together. When working with ratio goals, monitor your denominator to ensure accuracy, similar to calibrating your microscope. For absolute goals, track both the conversion rate and upstream funnel to gain a panoramic view that complements the detailed landscape beneath it.

GOAL TYPE	PROS	CONS
Absolute Goal (e.g., Total Revenue, DAU)	Directly tied to business outcomes	Heavily influenced by external factors
	Easy to understand and communicate	Hard to isolate team impact
	Clear impact on company success	May fluctuate due to upstream changes
Ratio Goal (e.g., Conversion Rate, Retention %)	Better isolates team impact	Still affected by user mix changes
	More stable across volume changes	Can be harder to interpret
	Good for measuring efficiency	May mask absolute impact size

Table 9-1: Pros and cons of different types of goals

WHAT ARE EFFECTIVE GOALS?

Every successful product journey begins with clear, well-defined goals. This framework outlines how to set effective product goals that drive meaningful impact.

Effective metrics embody four key principles:

1. **Mission alignment:** Each metric must directly reflect your product's purpose and strategic direction. Clearly articulate your mission to ensure alignment.
2. **Interpretability:** Metrics should be clear enough for everyone, from engineers to executives, to understand without explanation.
3. **Actionability:** Metrics must guide tangible improvements and inform daily decisions. Ensure that metrics are responsive enough to reflect changes within a reasonable time frame, especially during experiments.

4. **Integrity:** Metrics must discourage manipulative behavior, such as pure click-through rate optimization that fosters clickbait tactics. Consider the following example:

SUBSCRIPTION REVENUE GROWTH

- **Aligned with mission:** Focusing on recurring revenue supports the goal of building a sustainable, customer-centric business model.
- **Clearly understood:** A target of 15 percent growth in subscription revenue is straightforward and motivating for teams across the organization.
- **Actionable direction:** Teams can concentrate on specific areas for improvement, such as enhancing onboarding processes, personalizing plans, or boosting retention strategies.

BEYOND PRIMARY GOALS: THE ART OF BALANCED METRICS

Imagine building a house. While the primary goal is to create a beautiful home, you must also ensure it is structurally sound, energy-efficient, and safe. Similarly, in product development, focusing solely on primary goals proves insufficient. A holistic approach is essential to ensure a healthy and sustainable path to success.

This is where counter metrics and guardrail metrics come into play—think of them as your product's vital signs and safety measures.

Counter Metrics: The Balance Keepers

Counter metrics serve as a system of checks and balances, ensuring that progress toward your main goal does not compromise other crucial aspects of your product. Consider the following metrics in the context of a recommendation system:

1. **Usability metrics:** Just as a beautiful house needs functional doors and windows, track how easily users interact with recommendations through click-through rates and navigation patterns.
2. **Performance metrics:** Like monitoring a home's electrical and plumbing systems, keep an eye on system latency and uptime to ensure smooth operation.
3. **Quality metrics:** Similar to conducting regular home inspections, use precision and recall measurements to verify the accuracy and relevance of recommendations.

These metrics work together to ensure that while you improve recommendation accuracy, you also maintain a high-quality user experience.

Guardrail Metrics: The Safety Net

Think of guardrail metrics as your product's ethical compass and safety protocols. For example, in a recommendation system, consider the following:

1. **Content diversity:** Ensure recommendations do not create echo chambers, similar to maintaining a balanced diet instead of only eating your favorite food.
2. **Transparency:** Ensure users understand and trust recom-

mendations, much like providing clear labels on medicine bottles.

3. **Safety standards:** Maintain strict content quality controls, similar to installing safety rails on a steep staircase.

In monetization, adopting this balanced approach is even more important. Consider these real-world examples:

- **Goal metric:** Increase subscription revenue by 15 percent.
- **Counter metrics:** Keep churn under 5 percent and loading times under one second.
- **Guardrail metrics:** Maintain NPS above seventy and refund rates below 2 percent.

By integrating these various types of metrics, you create a robust framework that drives growth while safeguarding what matters most: user trust, product quality, and long-term sustainability.

PUTTING A NUMBER TO YOUR GOAL METRIC: CHARTING YOUR COURSE TO SUCCESS

Setting targets is like reaching for the stars—distant yet inspiring, pushing us beyond our limits. Astronomers carefully calculate the trajectories to reach celestial bodies; similarly, you must balance ambition with achievability. Aiming for a distant star and reaching the moon feels more motivating than targeting a nearby mountain and merely hitting its peak. However, setting an unrealistic goal like reaching another galaxy may discourage the team from even embarking on the journey. Generally, targets are set with an 80 percent or 50 percent chance the team can reach the target.

Effective goal setting requires both art and science. Like a meteorologist forecasting weather patterns, analyze potential outcomes based on the current trajectory—referred to as business as usual (BAU). This analysis may involve plotting historical growth trends or employing sophisticated predictive models that consider seasonal patterns, market dynamics, and user behavior.

Successful organizations typically adopt a two-pronged approach for meaningful target setting:

THE TOP-DOWN PERSPECTIVE: ALIGNING VISION WITH REALITY

Just like a ship's captain charting a course through unknown waters, company leadership must provide strategic direction grounded in market opportunities and stakeholder expectations. For example, the board may establish an ambitious target of 20 percent year-over-year growth to strengthen their market position.

THE BOTTOM-UP APPROACH: BUILDING FROM THE GROUND UP

Individual teams assess their specific domains, much like expedition teams exploring various routes up a mountain. They evaluate their capabilities, planned initiatives, and potential improvements. The product leader encourages teams to establish "stretch achievable" goals—ambitious enough to spark innovation, but realistic enough to sustain momentum.

A REAL-WORLD EXAMPLE

Let me share how the recommendation team approached their ambitious goal of a 20 percent improvement. They developed a comprehensive strategy that would build upon itself, like chapters in a compelling story:

1. **Building the foundation (+5 percent improvement):** Like a master chef selecting quality ingredients, the team began by gathering rich data. They combined insights from web clicks, app interactions, and in-store purchases to create a detailed tapestry of customer behavior. This solid foundation alone promised a 5 percent boost in recommendation accuracy.

2. **Unleashing AI's potential (+6 percent improvement):** Next, the team introduced sophisticated AI models—imagine thousands of digital personal shoppers learning from every customer interaction. This new deep learning system could understand product relationships so effectively that it could improve recommendation relevance by 6 percent.

3. **Adding the personal touch (+4 percent improvement):** The system learned to read contextual cues, behaving like a thoughtful friend who knows precisely what you need. Breakfast suggestions in the morning and umbrella recommendations on rainy days enhanced engagement, contributing a 4 percent improvement.

4. **Fine-tuning the experience (+2 percent improvement):** Through systematic A/B testing, the team refined their approach. Each test of placement and format was like adjusting a lens for the perfect focus, resulting in a 2 percent increase in click-through rates.

5. **Racing against time (+2 percent improvement):** Speed became the next frontier. By reducing recommendation

updates from five minutes to instantaneous, the team captured fleeting moments of customer interest, raising conversion rates by an additional 2 percent.

6. **Listening to our customers (+1 percent improvement):** No story is complete without customer feedback. By establishing direct channels for user input, the team fine-tuned recommendations, achieving that final 1 percent to reach their 20 percent goal.

FINDING THE SWEET SPOT

The magic occurs when these approaches converge. Historical data indicates that a 15 percent improvement is achievable through planned enhancements, while the top-down target stands at 20 percent. Instead of seeing this as a gap, the team recognizes it as an opportunity for innovation—whether by launching new features or optimizing existing processes.

When exploring uncharted territory without historical data, the team turns to industry benchmarks and similar success stories for guidance. This process is like planning an expedition to a newly discovered peak, where studying comparable mountains and learning from others' experiences informs the overall strategy.

TRACKING PROGRESS: BUILDING A CULTURE OF ACCOUNTABILITY

With clear goals established, the next crucial step is implementing a robust tracking system. Effective goal tracking, much like a well-oiled machine, demands routine maintenance and rapid response capabilities. Successful organizations maintain visibility and drive results through a combination of proactive monitoring and swift reaction to deviations.

PROACTIVE APPROACH: STAYING AHEAD OF THE CURVE

1. **Weekly pulse checks:**
   A. Data scientists compile comprehensive dashboards for leadership, offering real-time insights into goal progression. These reports highlight key metrics, emerging trends, and data-driven recommendations for optimizing performance.
2. **Monthly strategic reviews:**
   A. Cross-functional teams convene to assess progress across all metrics—from high-level goals to guardrail indicators. These collaborative sessions foster alignment and enable timely course corrections.

REACTIVE APPROACH: RESPONDING WITH PRECISION

1. **Smart monitoring systems:**
   A. Automated alerts flag significant metric deviations (typically beyond 10 percent of target), facilitating the quick escalation of critical issues that require immediate attention.
2. **Root cause analysis:**
   A. Analytics teams conduct thorough investigations into performance anomalies, examining factors ranging from technical issues to external market influences.
   B. Findings translate into actionable solutions, addressing technical debt, adjusting feature priorities, or implementing tactical fixes.

3. Swift resolution protocol:
   A. Cross-functional teams collaborate to implement necessary changes, ensuring metrics align with their target trajectory while maintaining product quality and user experience.

THE DYNAMIC NATURE OF GOAL SETTING: AN EVOLVING JOURNEY

Setting goals is not a one-time event; it is an ongoing process that requires constant refinement and collaboration. As the business landscape shifts and new insights emerge, goals must adapt accordingly, whether through adjusting metrics for different time frames or recalibrating targets midcourse.

THE EVOLUTION OF GOALS ACROSS COMPANY LIFE CYCLES

Consider your company a growing organism, with each stage of development demanding its own unique focus and metrics:

Early Stage: Finding Your Roots

In the early stage, like a seedling breaking through soil, startups must focus intently on achieving product market fit. Success hinges on fundamental questions: Do users return? Do they become engaged and become advocates? These critical signals reveal whether your product has found fertile ground.

Growth Stage: Branching Out

As your company gains momentum, goals naturally shift beyond pure growth. Like a maturing tree developing a robust root system, focus expands to optimizing resource allocation. Key metrics include customer acquisition costs and tracking efficiency alongside growth indicators.

Maturity Stage: Creating an Ecosystem

At the maturity stage, established companies function like keystone species in a forest, where success relies on maintaining a delicate balance. Goals at this level integrate multiple dimensions: sustainable growth, operational excellence, market leadership, and innovation, all while maintaining profitability and customer satisfaction.

THE ART OF GOAL RECALIBRATION

Markets shift and assumptions change. Successful organizations recognize when it's time to adjust their course. Instead of clinging to unrealistic targets, effective teams routinely re-forecast monthly, especially in response to unexpected market dynamics or overly optimistic initial projections.

CROSS-FUNCTIONAL COLLABORATION: THE KEY TO MEANINGFUL GOALS

Setting effective goals demands a symphony of perspectives. While data scientists analyze the metrics, product teams ensure targets align with user needs, and engineering validates technical feasibility. Various departments must coordinate these efforts. For example, in a product-led growth initiative, success relies on marketing driving awareness while product teams develop features that facilitate viral sharing and smart onboarding. This collaborative approach ensures that goals are not only ambitious but also achievable through unified effort.

TAKEAWAY

Effective goal setting is the cornerstone of product success. Here's what you need to know:

1. **Set SMART goals:** Ensure your goals are specific, measurable, achievable, relevant, and time-bound.
2. **Balance your metrics:** Combine growth metrics, counter metrics, and guardrail metrics to promote sustainable progress.
3. **Stay flexible:** Adapt your goals as your product evolves, emphasizing what matters most at each stage.
4. **Track and adjust:** Regularly monitor progress and make data-informed adjustments when necessary.

Remember: the best goals strike a balance between ambition and achievability. They should challenge your team while remaining within reach, always prioritizing user value and business objectives.

EXERCISE

Let's practice goal setting with a real-world scenario: you are the product leader for a mobile banking app, and you need to set goals for the next quarter.

GIVEN DATA

- Current Monthly Active Users (MAU): 500,000
- Current user engagement rate: 45 percent
- App store rating: 4.2/5.0
- Average transaction completion rate: 88 percent
- Customer support tickets per one thousand users: fifteen

QUESTIONS

Question 1: Set a primary goal metric for user growth. Consider:

- Historical growth rate of 5 percent month-over-month
- Recent launch of new features
- Competitor growth rates of 8–10 percent

Question 2: Define at least three counter metrics to ensure balanced growth.

Question 3: Establish two guardrail metrics to protect core product value.

Question 4: Break down your primary goal into specific initiatives, estimating the impact of each.

Question 5: Create a weekly tracking plan that includes:

- Key metrics to monitor
- Threshold for alerts
- Action plan if metrics deviate from targets

This exercise will help you apply this chapter's frameworks

to a realistic scenario while practicing the balance between ambition and achievability in goal setting.

ANSWERS

Question 1: Set a primary goal metric for user growth. Consider:

- Historical growth rate of 5 percent month-over-month
- Recent launch of new features
- Competitor growth rates of 8–10 percent

Answer: Primary Goal Metric:

Increase MAU by 25 percent (reaching 625,000) over the next quarter.

Question 2: Define at least three counter metrics to ensure balanced growth.

Answer: Counter Metrics:

- Maintain user engagement rate above 42 percent.
- Keep app load time under two seconds.
- Maintain transaction completion rate above 85 percent.

Question 3: Establish two guardrail metrics to protect core product value.

Answer: Guardrail Metrics:

- Keep app store rating above 4.0.

- Keep customer support tickets below twenty per one thousand users.

Question 4: Break down your primary goal into specific initiatives, estimating the impact of each.

Answer: Goal Breakdown Initiatives:

- Referral program optimization (+8 percent MAU)
  ○ Improve referral flow UX.
  ○ Increase referral rewards.
- New user onboarding improvements (+7 percent MAU)
  ○ Simplified registration process.
  ○ Interactive tutorial improvements.
- Feature awareness campaign (+6 percent MAU)
  ○ In-app notifications.
  ○ Email engagement series.
- Paid acquisition optimization (+4 percent MAU)
  ○ Refined targeting.
  ○ Creative optimization.

Question 5: Create a weekly tracking plan that includes:

- Key metrics to monitor
- Thresholds for alerts
- Action plan if metrics deviate from targets

Answer: Weekly Tracking Plan:

- **Key Metrics to Monitor:**
  ○ Daily/Weekly MAU growth rate
  ○ User engagement metrics

- Conversion rates at each funnel stage
- **Alert Thresholds:**
  - 10 percent deviation from weekly growth targets
  - 5 percent drop in engagement rates
  - 15 percent increase in support tickets
- **Action Plan for Deviations:**
  - Immediate team review meeting for metrics outside thresholds
  - Root cause analysis within twenty-four hours
  - Adjustment of initiatives based on findings
  - Weekly progress reviews with stakeholders

Notes

1. **Mission:** Help creators build a community online
2. **Human language goal:** Increase follower count for creators on our platform
3. **Metric:** Number of followers in twenty-eight days
4. **Target:** Total one million follows

Chapter 10

DESIGN AND IMPLEMENT EFFECTIVE EXPERIMENTS

THE ROLE OF EXPERIMENTATION IN PRODUCT GROWTH
EXPERIMENTATION MOVES THE TEAM FROM INSIGHTS TO ACTION

In the previous chapters, you learned how to identify growth opportunities through a deep dive into your data. You pinpointed areas where your product shines and where optimization is feasible. However, identifying these opportunities is just the beginning. To drive effective growth with confidence and ensure team alignment, validate your hypotheses with solid evidence. This is where experimentation, particularly A/B testing, is essential, enabling you to transition from insights to action.

ALL USEFUL ANALYSES ARE CAUSAL ANALYSES

You may wonder, *What about prediction models, growth accounting, or funnel analysis? Aren't those focused on correlations, rather than causation?* While this is true, your primary responsibility as a data analyst or a data scientist is to establish clear causal claims. You must be able to assert, "Based on my analysis, I recommend pursuing A instead of B, because I believe A will attract more users, boost engagement, or increase revenue." Essentially, you are saying, "This change will *cause* that outcome."

Thus, all valuable analyses should aim to demonstrate a causal relationship. When strong causal evidence exists, the path forward is clear. If not, it's your responsibility to build a convincing argument that your recommendation will positively impact the business.

Data can be highly persuasive, but only when presented clearly and supported by sound reasoning. This is why experimentation—specifically randomized controlled trials, the gold standard of A/B testing—is crucial for product growth. These experiments provide the strongest possible evidence to support your decisions. While other ways to gather insights exist, make experiments your default approach whenever possible.

A QUICK INTRODUCTION TO RANDOMIZED CONTROL TRIALS AND CAUSAL INFERENCE

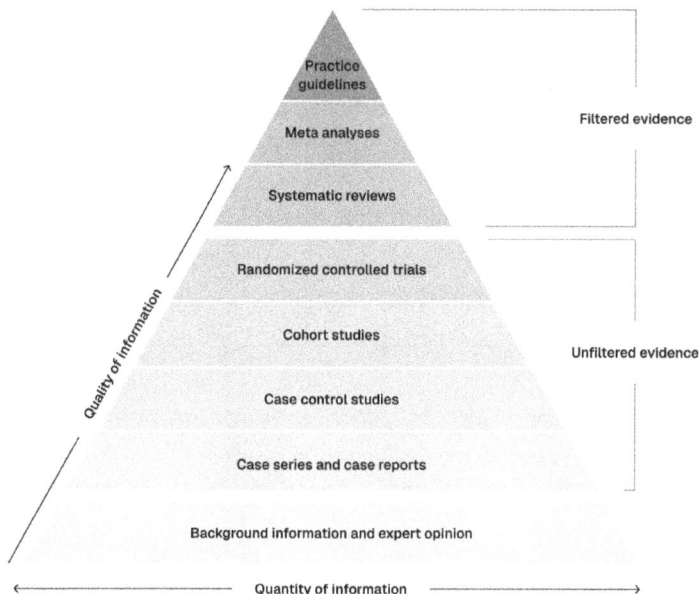

Figure 10-1: The Evidence Pyramid (Source: "The Evidence Pyriamid," University of New England, accessed July 8, 2025, https://library.une.edu/research-help/help-with/evidence-based-practice/the-evidence-pyramid/).

The evidence pyramid ranks types of studies according to their strength and reliability. At the pinnacle are randomized controlled trials (RCTs), considered the most rigorous form of unfiltered evidence. Results from well-conducted A/B tests should take precedence over other forms of evidence due to their high reliability.

Consider the following example. You want to change the messaging on a call-to-action (CTA) button from "Purchase" to "Buy Now" with the aim of boosting conversion rates. Here's a step-by-step application of the evidence pyramid:

1. **Expert opinions:** Consult professionals to determine whether this change is likely to be effective.
2. **Case studies:** Review case studies or other businesses that implemented similar changes to their CTA buttons.
3. **Data analysis:** Systematically analyze data to identify patterns comparing buttons labeled "Purchase" and "Buy Now."
4. **Cohort studies:** Implement the change from the "Purchase" button to "Buy Now," then monitor conversion rates before and after the change.
5. **Randomized controlled trial (RCT):** Randomly assign half the users to see the "Purchase" button, while the other half observes the "Buy Now" button. Compare the conversion rates between these two groups.

By following these steps, you can ensure that your decision-making process is grounded in the strongest available evidence.

Each step builds on the previous one by addressing potential biases:

1. **Transition from expert opinion to case studies:** Experts can be wrong or biased, so seek patterns in real-world cases to inform decisions.
2. **Transition from case studies to systematic comparisons:** Because case studies may not be relevant to your customers or your circumstances, conduct comparisons to gain broader insights.
3. **Transition from comparisons to cohort studies:** Comparisons alone cannot determine whether changes in outcomes result from the intervention or from other factors, such as seasonality or external events.

4. **Transition from cohort studies to RCTs:** Only RCTs, such as A/B testing, can adequately control for all variables. With random assignment, you can confidently attribute differences between groups to the treatment—in this case, changing "Purchase" to "Buy Now."

The effectiveness of A/B testing lies in two key principles:

1. **Random assignment:** By randomly assigning one group to experience the change (button "Buy Now") and another to remain unchanged (button "Purchase"), any differences in results (such as age, income, height, and conversion rate on your call to action) can be attributed to the treatment rather than external factors or chance.
2. **The law of large numbers:** When a sufficiently large sample size is randomly split into two groups, their average traits (e.g., age, income, height, and conversion rate on your call to action) will be statistically similar.

A/B testing offers exceptional value because it requires no additional assumptions beyond following proper procedures. Conduct rigorous tests to obtain the most reliable evidence possible. If A/B testing is an option, use it—it's the gold standard for making evidence-based decisions.

KEY FACTORS FOR SUCCESSFUL EXPERIMENTATION

Successful product growth teams excel at the 80/20 rule, recognizing that 20 percent of their efforts can yield 80 percent of the results. The focus remains on the vital few rather than the trivial many. This principle applies to experimentation as well.

Consider the following critical elements:

- **Clear hypothesis:** Define what you are testing and why.
- **Solid infrastructure:**
  - **Balanced groups:** Ensure test and control groups are truly comparable.
  - **Accurate logging:** Track relevant data accurately and effectively.
  - **Easy setup:** Create tests quickly and effortlessly.
  - **Comprehensive metrics:** Monitor a wide range of metrics efficiently.
- **Culture of experimentation:**
  - **Openness to ideas:** Empower every team member to suggest experiments.
  - **Collaborative decisions:** Foster a team-based approach to decision-making rather than top-down directives.
  - **Humility:** Accept that most initial ideas may not produce the expected outcomes.
  - **Celebrate learning:** Emphasize lessons learned from each experiment, regardless of whether the outcome is a "success" or a "failure."
  - **Iterative development:** Continuously refine the product based on experimental results.

Avoid getting bogged down in the intricate statistical details, which are important but warrant a separate discussion, such as in the book *Trustworthy Online Controlled Experiments*. This chapter focuses on the big picture: what scalable experimentation entails and why it serves as a game-changer for product growth. To grasp the importance of experiments, first recognize how often initial ideas miss the mark.

EMBRACE BEING WRONG: WHY MOST IDEAS INITIALLY FAIL

A significant gap exists in how people perceive their own ideas. Those who run experiments regularly understand the value of humility regarding their initial hypotheses because they witness how often they fall short. Research indicates that around 80 percent of initial ideas fail to deliver the expected results, across various companies and teams.[4] In contrast, individuals who seldom experiment typically overestimate the success rates of their ideas.

Accepting this reality can be challenging. To understand why this is the case, consider the following two main reasons:

1. **Tackling difficult problems:** If ideas succeeded most of the time, it would mean that we're dealing with simpler issues. However, product growth operates at the forefront of product development, marketing, and industry best practices. There are no guarantees that any idea will work perfectly on the first attempt.
2. **Complexity of modern products:** The ecosystem surrounding today's products is extraordinarily intricate. This complexity overwhelms the human brain's capacity to fully comprehend every aspect simultaneously.

The first point is intuitive, while the second one is more nuanced. To illustrate this complexity, consider the story of DDT and bald eagles as an analogy.

---

4   Ron Kohavi, "Succes Rate of Ideas vs. Experiments and the Implications of False Positive Statistically Significant Results," Google Doc Publication, December 10, 2023, https://docs.google.com/document/d/1_D2IslIR9HsdGpOg3J1g44G5VqfTkTVw/edit; Ron Kohavi, Thomas Crook, and Roger Longbotham, "Online Experimentation at Microsoft," Microsoft Experimentation Platform, Redmond, Washington: Microsoft, 2009. https://exp-platform.com/Documents/ExP_DMCaseStudies.pdf; Lenny Rachitsky, "Love these stats from Ronny Kohavi on the...," LinkedIn, 2023, https://www.linkedin.com/posts/lennyrachitsky_love-these-stats-from-ronny-kohavi-on-the-activity-7093034038566809600-cGDa.

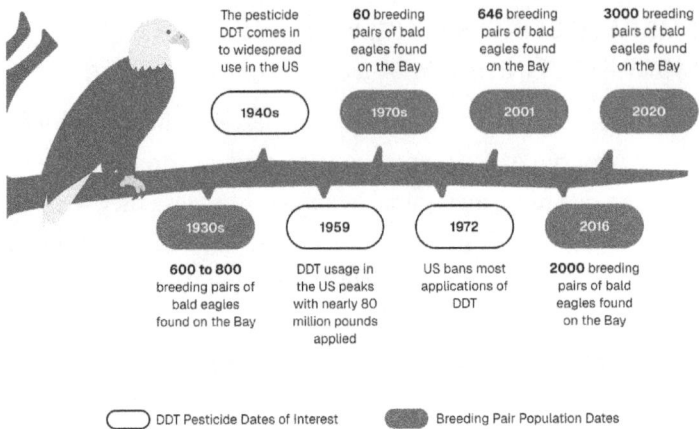

Figure 10-2: DDT and bald eagles statistics

In the 1940s, scientists celebrated DDT as a breakthrough pesticide, impressed by its remarkable effectiveness and concluding, after extensive research, that it posed no significant environmental risk.

However, the consequences emerged years later. Bald eagles were indirectly harmed by DDT after consuming contaminated fish. As the pesticide moved up the food chain, it became increasingly concentrated, weakening eagle eggshells. This fragility caused eggs to break easily during incubation, leading to a sharp decline in the eagle population.

Looking back, the connection seems obvious, but no one at the time could have foreseen the complex ripple effects triggered by DDT. Modern products often face similarly intricate challenges: markets are diverse, user needs vary widely, and products themselves can be extraordinarily complex. Acknowledging this reality requires humility in how we approach predictions and an understanding that outcomes may differ significantly from expectations.

Once you accept these realities, the necessity of experimentation for achieving sustainable, compounding growth becomes clear. Understanding what works, what does not, and how to make improvements is essential for success.

Don't mistake motion with progress

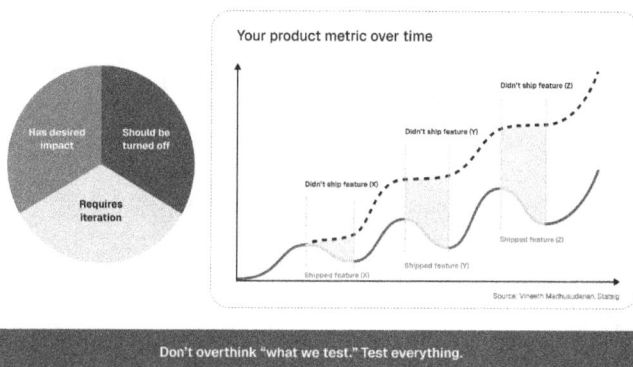

Figure 10-3: Mistaking motion with progress

To better internalize the ideas behind experimentation, consider the following real-life examples.

EXAMPLE ONE: SHIFTING THE PRIORITY OF MARKETPLACE PRODUCT WITH A/B TESTING

My conviction about A/B testing solidified during an attempt to promote e-commerce on a marketplace product within a social app during the COVID-19 pandemic. We initially failed, but through a pivot, we eventually achieved success.

A/B TESTING REVEALED THE FAILURE

Marketplace seemed like a natural fit for e-commerce since users frequently shopped there. Our product leader came from eBay, and we recruited teams from companies like Walmart.

These teams entered war rooms to create an e-commerce-first experience on Marketplace.

Coming from Amazon, I was excited about the initiative and willingly worked many overnight shifts.

The first major launch on the main tab featured a well-thought-out design with a modern aesthetic, seamless checkout flow, and dedicated teams curating attractive and relevant selections. We also matched competitors' prices with subsidies and offered generous return policies.

Fortunately, we conducted an A/B test for the launch, which revealed a disastrous outcome. The result shocked everyone, including me.

The test revealed declines in nearly every metric: conversion rates from the product detail page to checkout, click-through rates from browse to the product detail page, the number of browse impressions, and Daily Active Users.

It was clear: *Marketplace users hated what we launched.*

When a failure occurs, two primary reasons typically emerge: either the concept is flawed, or the execution of the idea fails. Naturally, leaders questioned the execution—and justifiably so. I questioned our execution as well.

ANALYZING THE FAILURE THROUGH EXPERIMENTS

Fortunately, another experiment helped the team avoid pursuing a doomed idea and facing repercussions for its failure.

The experiment was designed to provide strong evidence that e-commerce simply does not work on Marketplace. Our hypothesis suggested that Marketplace users are specifically seeking deals; they are just not generally interested in e-commerce products.

In hindsight, this makes sense: Why would users buy an e-commerce product from a social app when they can rely on Amazon? However, how could we convince those determined to make e-commerce successful on our platform?

THE IMPACT OF A WHITE BACKGROUND

We discovered that most "Marketplace native" products feature in-context backgrounds with their product images—like displaying an item on a table—while most e-commerce products use plain, professional white backgrounds.

To test this, we randomized the backgrounds of a consistent set of products, displaying either a white background image or an in-context image on the browse feed. Our findings showed that the white background led to decreases in both click-through and conversion rates: users felt as if they were in a traditional e-commerce experience rather than browsing for deals.

$30
LED light therapy mask
Bellevue, WA

$30
LED light therapy mask
Bellevue, WA

Figure 10-4: The two variants: Which one feels more like an e-commerce experience?

THE IMPACT OF A/B TESTING

The significance of A/B testing resonated deeply with me.

Before the white background experiment, I endured countless meetings filled with debates over which ideas would succeed, who was responsible for poor executions, and how to improve our processes.

After the white background experiment, those debates quickly concluded. We redirected our efforts toward enabling shipping for Marketplace local listings and achieved a twenty-six-time increase in online transactions on Marketplace over the next six months—outperforming similar social shopping apps combined.

Without these two experiments, many people's careers or lives would have been negatively affected.

At times, it feels as if leaders become villains in these narratives: poor strategy, misguided decisions, a lack of understanding of the business, and shifting blame to direct reports.

However, upon conducting an honest postmortem, I realized my perspective shifted midway through the journey. It's challenging to recognize reality when you are fully immersed in making an idea work.

To me, that's the true power of causal evidence and A/B testing: I believe even Mark Zuckerberg himself could not have convinced me more effectively.

EXAMPLE TWO: CAN LOWER-QUALITY VIDEO INCREASE REVENUE?

Vijaye Raji, former VP and Head of Entertainment at Facebook, shared an intriguing story about how a seemingly negative change in video quality yielded unexpectedly positive results. This experience emphasized the critical role of experimentation and challenging assumptions in product development.

THE COVID-19 CHALLENGE

During the COVID-19 pandemic, people turned to video for entertainment and connection, which significantly increased internet usage. This surge strained internet infrastructure and threatened essential online services. Governments and telecommunication companies urged video platforms to reduce bandwidth consumption.

THE COUNTERINTUITIVE SOLUTION

In response, an engineering team, led by Vijaye, decided to experiment with reducing video quality to decrease bandwidth usage. Their goal was to quantify the impact of reduced video quality on watch time and ad revenue. They anticipated a decline, as the organization had heavily invested in the belief that users prefer higher-quality videos. Past experiments consistently showed that better video quality led to increased watch time and ad revenue.

THE SURPRISING RESULTS

To their astonishment, the experiment yielded unexpected results. Although bandwidth usage decreased as intended, both watch time and ad revenue increased instead of declining. This counterintuitive outcome prompted further investigation. *Had the entire organization been wrong all along? What about all the engineering and hardware resources invested in enhancing video quality?*

THE ROOT CAUSE

In some organizations, leadership may choose to ignore negative results or bury them. Fortunately, Vijaye prioritized uncovering the truth. He assembled a dedicated data science team to investigate. By meticulously analyzing experiment results and comparing them with other analytics, the team quickly identified the root cause.

They discovered that during the pandemic, users, particularly in developing countries like India, faced usage quotas set by their carriers. By watching lower-quality videos, users could consume more content, which ultimately led to increased overall watch time and ad revenue.

THE POWER OF EXPERIMENTATION

In hindsight, could engineers have anticipated the impact of usage quotas? It's a challenging task. Similar to the insights gained from the bald eagle and DDT story, it's impossible for anyone to foresee every variable. This is why experimentation is essential. However, the value of successful experimentation must be rooted in a truth-seeking culture. I hope this story serves as a reminder that experimentation can uncover unexpected insights and drive product growth, especially in dynamic situations.

A DEEP DIVE INTO SCALABLE EXPERIMENTATION
WHAT IS SCALABLE EXPERIMENTATION?

Scalable experimentation involves making experimentation the default practice rather than the exception. Modern software development techniques, particularly feature flags and CI/CD (continuous integration/continuous delivery), have made this approach not only feasible but also optimal.

Consider the following: with feature flags, you can control when and to whom a new feature is released. This allows you to separate the act of deploying code from the process of changing a feature's configuration or visibility. This separation is a fundamental principle of modern software development.

With feature flags in place, you already have the foundation for scalable experiments. You have complete control over which users experience different versions of your product. By incorporating randomization, you create a system where experimentation becomes the norm rather than an isolated event.

We've identified seven key criteria for a scalable experimentation infrastructure. Use these to assess your own system:

1. **Define metrics once and use them everywhere:** Eliminate the need to reinvent the wheel for each experiment.
2. **Ensure reliable and transparent data:** Establish clarity so everyone understands the data's meaning and origin.
3. **Build, test, and deploy the same code:** Reduce the risk of introducing errors when launching experiments.
4. **Foster a culture of experimentation:** Make experimentation an integral part of your team's DNA (refer to the "Best Practices for Building an Experimentation Culture" section that follows).
5. **Provide clear, layered information:** Present data in an easily understandable format to support informed decision-making.
6. **Utilize a trustworthy and practical statistical engine:** Avoid overly complex statistical methods that are difficult to interpret.
7. **Automate wherever possible:** Streamline the process by automating logging, health checks, calculations, experiment management, and any other tasks.

Default-on Experimentation:
Feature flags + Stats engine = Experiments

Architecture feature flag and experiment as the same object

1. Feature flags: Implement conditional rules

2. Stats engine: Analyze impact
  - Randomly split users into different feature experience
  - Bring existing metrics

We get experiment readout natively.

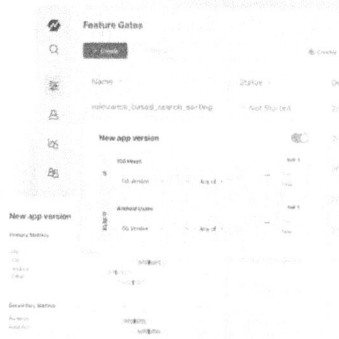

Key technical insights:
Experiments = feature toggles + randomization

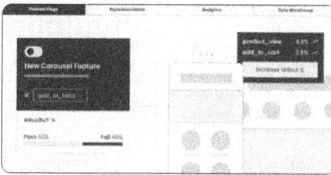

Feature flags

If x then A
If not x then B
Control x% in console

Experiments

Experiments = Feature flags + randomization + metrics

Figure 10-5: How to have default-on experimentation

WHY IS SCALABLE EXPERIMENTATION NECESSARY?

Experiments are incredibly valuable, but they're not "necessary" in the same way that using Excel for basic accounting is. Experiments focus on discovering new growth opportunities rather than maintaining the status quo. They belong in the classic "important, but not urgent" category.

To integrate experimentation into your regular workflow, you must eliminate as many barriers as possible. This requires investing in the right infrastructure. Consider it this way: you could walk to a distant river daily to fetch water, or you could drill a well that provides a reliable water source for your entire village. The well demands an up-front investment, but it offers significant long-term benefits.

Experimentation is a skill developed through practice. Making it the default choice is crucial. If you do not, the cost—in terms of time and effort—of running and maintaining experiments will increase faster than your capacity to keep pace, ultimately causing your experimentation program to stall.

Scalable experimentation requires scalable infrastructure

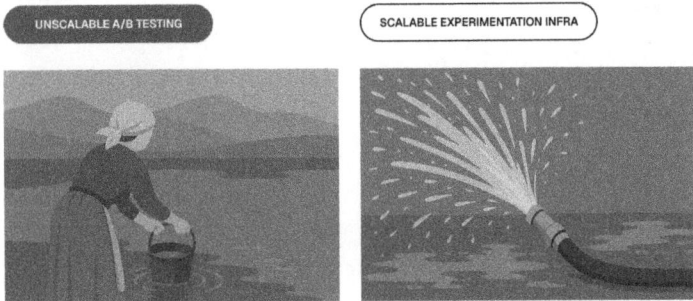

Figure 10-6: Scalable experimentation requires scalable infrastructure

In simple terms, experimentation is a craft that you can only master through practice. Therefore, it is essential to make experimentation your default choice. If you do not, the costs of running and maintaining additional experiments will increase dramatically, ultimately leading to failure.

TAKEAWAY

Here's a quick start table to guide you as you get started with scalable experimentation:

MEASURE	ANALYSES TO RUN	ACTIONS TO TAKE	YOU KNOW YOU ARE READY TO MOVE ON WHEN...
Current Experimentation Capabilities	Audit your existing tools and processes. Assess your team's understanding of experimentation. Identify bottlenecks in your current workflow.	Map out your ideal experimentation process. Research and select appropriate tools (feature flagging, A/B testing platforms). Develop training materials for your team.	You have a clear understanding of your current state, a vision for your future state, and a plan to bridge the gap.
Experimentation Infrastructure	Monitor the health of your feature flagging and A/B testing systems. Track key metrics related to experiment setup, execution, and analysis.	Automate as much of the experimentation process as possible. Establish clear guidelines for data quality and consistency.	Your experimentation infrastructure is reliable, efficient, and supports running multiple experiments concurrently.
Experimentation Culture	Survey your team to gauge their attitudes toward experimentation. Track the number of experiments proposed and launched by different team members.	Create a safe space for sharing ideas and learning from failures. Recognize and reward individuals and teams who champion experimentation.	Experimentation is a core part of your team's DNA, and everyone feels empowered to contribute.

MEASURE	ANALYSES TO RUN	ACTIONS TO TAKE	YOU KNOW YOU ARE READY TO MOVE ON WHEN...
Impact of Experimentation on Product Growth	Track the number of successful experiments that lead to product improvements. Measure the impact of these improvements on key business metrics.	Develop a system for documenting and sharing experiment results. Use experiment results to inform product strategy and road map prioritization.	You can demonstrate a clear link between your experimentation efforts and positive business outcomes. You have all graph mockups ready for the next iteration.

Table 10-1: Quick start scalable experimentation

EXERCISE

Do the following practical exercise to apply the concepts from this chapter:

QUESTIONS

You are working on a mobile app that has seen declining user engagement. Your team has hypothesized that app performance might be the issue.

Question 1: Experiment Design. Design an A/B test to investigate the impact of video quality on user engagement. Consider:

- What metrics will you track?
- How will you segment your users?
- What potential confounding variables should you control for?

Question 2: Data Analysis. Given the following hypothetical data from your experiment (assuming the experiment is sufficiently powered and the difference is statistically significant):

METRIC	CONTROL GROUP (HIGH QUALITY)	TEST GROUP (LOWER QUALITY)
Average session duration	8.5 minutes	12.3 minutes
Data usage per session	45MB	28MB
User retention (seven-day)	65 percent	72 percent

Table 10-2: Hypothetical data from your experiment

- Analyze this data and explain:
  - What conclusions can you draw?
  - What additional data would help strengthen your analysis?
  - How would you communicate these results to stakeholders?

Question 3: Implementation Plan. Based on your findings, create a plan:

- How would you implement the changes using feature flags?
- What monitoring systems would you put in place?
- How would you roll out the changes gradually?

Submit your answers with supporting data and reasoning. Remember to consider the principles of scalable experimentation discussed in this chapter.

ANSWERS

Question 1: Experiment Design. Design an A/B test to investigate the impact of video quality on user engagement. Consider:

- What metrics will you track?
- How will you segment your users?
- What potential confounding variables should you control for?

Answer: A well-designed experiment would include:

- **Key metrics:**
  - Primary: User engagement (session duration, retention)
  - Secondary: Data consumption, video completion rates
  - Guardrail: App crash rate, user complaints
- **Segmentation:**
  - By device type (to control for hardware differences)
  - By network connection type (Wi-Fi vs. cellular)
  - By geographic region (to account for infrastructure differences)
- **Controls for:**
  - Time of day variations
  - User demographics
  - Content type differences

Question 2: Data Analysis. Given the following hypothetical data from your experiment (assuming the experiment is sufficiently powered and the difference is statistically significant):

METRIC	CONTROL GROUP (HIGH QUALITY)	TEST GROUP (LOWER QUALITY)
Average session duration	8.5 minutes	12.3 minutes
Data usage per session	45MB	28MB
User retention (seven-day)	65 percent	72 percent

Table 10-2: Hypothetical data from your experiment

- Analyze this data and explain:
  - What conclusions can you draw?
  - What additional data would help strengthen your analysis?
  - How would you communicate these results to stakeholders?

Answer: Based on the provided data, we can conclude:

- **Positive impacts:**
  - 45 percent increase in session duration (8.5 to 12.3 minutes)
  - 38 percent reduction in data usage (45MB to 28MB)
  - 7 percent improvement in retention (65 percent to 72 percent)
- Additional data needed:
  - User satisfaction scores
  - Long-term retention metrics (thirty-day, ninety-day)
  - Revenue impact

Question 3: Implementation Plan. Based on your findings, create a plan:

- How would you implement the changes using feature flags?

- What monitoring systems would you put in place?
- How would you roll out the changes gradually?

Answer: A robust implementation plan would include:

- **Feature flag strategy:**
  - Create granular flags for different quality levels.
  - Implement user-level override capability.
  - Build automatic quality adjustment based on network conditions.
- **Monitoring system:**
  - Real-time dashboards for key metrics.
  - Automated alerts for anomaly detection.
  - User feedback collection system.
- **Gradual rollout plan:**
  - Week one: 5 percent of users.
  - Week two: 20 percent of users if no issues.
  - Week three through four: Ramp to 50 percent while monitoring metrics.
  - Week five and beyond: Full rollout if metrics remain positive.

CONCLUSION

THE JOURNEY CONTINUES

As we reach the end of this *Growth Data Analytics Playbook*, we hope you are equipped with the frameworks, methodologies, and practical insights needed to drive meaningful growth for your product. The path from data to decisions is rarely linear, but with the right analytical mindset, it becomes increasingly navigable.

Remember this fundamental truth: growth is not a noun—it's a verb. It's an ongoing process that evolves as a company moves through different stages. There's no one-size-fits-all growth strategy. Every company's path depends on its product, market, business model, and maturity. But one thing remains constant: the importance of analytics and data.

APPLYING WHAT YOU HAVE LEARNED

Data is the foundation that helps you form hypotheses about what might be driving—or stalling—growth. It surfaces insights, reveals hidden levers, and guides decision-making. Once your product is past the minimum viable product (MVP) stage and has been in-market for a while, it's especially valuable to revisit the growth accounting framework—to identify the weakest link in your user journey or growth funnel.

Throughout this book, we've provided tools and techniques to help you deeply diagnose those problem areas—whether it's activation, retention, or reactivation—and take action with confidence. When you are unsure whether a change will move the needle, experimentation becomes your best tool for understanding causality.

We encourage you to approach the concepts in this playbook not as rigid rules but as adaptable frameworks. Every product is unique, with its own set of challenges and opportunities. The most successful growth organizations are those who can blend analytical rigor with creative problem-solving, tailoring approaches to their specific context.

Remember that growth analytics is as much about asking the right questions as it is about finding the right answers. Cultivate curiosity, challenge assumptions, and always tie your analyses back to user value and business impact.

THE EVOLUTION OF GROWTH ANALYTICS IN THE AGE OF ARTIFICIAL INTELLIGENCE

The field of growth analytics continues to evolve rapidly, with new tools, methodologies, and best practices emerging regularly. Artificial intelligence (AI) is dramatically transforming this landscape, enabling deeper insights through advanced pattern recognition, automated analysis, and predictive modeling. AI-powered tools now help identify user behavior patterns that would be impossible to detect manually, automate complex segmentation, and generate actionable growth recommendations in real time.

As data becomes increasingly abundant and accessible, the competitive advantage will shift to those who can leverage AI to extract meaningful signals from the noise and translate those signals into strategic action. Growth teams equipped with AI capabilities can test hypotheses faster, personalize user experiences at scale, and identify growth opportunities before they become obvious to competitors.

Even when growth is trending upward, it's worth asking: *How fast is fast enough?* A goal-oriented mindset enables teams to prioritize effectively, balance short-term wins with long-term investments, and stay aligned on outcomes that matter—both for the business and for the people behind it. AI tools can support this process by running countless scenario analyses and helping teams make more informed strategic decisions.

FINAL THOUGHTS

We began this playbook by emphasizing the crucial role that growth analytics plays in scaling products. We end with a reminder that behind every data point is a user—a person with needs, preferences, and behaviors. The most powerful growth strategies are those that align business objectives with genuine user value.

Thank you for joining us on this journey through the world of growth analytics. We hope this playbook serves as a valuable reference as you navigate the challenges and opportunities of growing your product. The path forward may not always be clear, but with data as your guide and user value as your North Star, you are well-equipped to make informed decisions that drive sustainable growth.

Ultimately, growth is not just about momentum—it's about *intentional progress*, driven by insight, aligned with purpose, and executed with discipline.

Now, it's time to put these concepts into practice. Here's to your continued success in leveraging analytics to unlock new dimensions of growth!

ABOUT THE AUTHORS

MENGYING LI is a data science leader and growth strategist with over a decade of experience driving impact at some of the world's most influential tech companies. She currently leads data strategy and product-led growth (PLG) at Braintrust, building on prior roles at MotherDuck, Notion, Meta, and Microsoft. A trusted advisor to early stage startups, Mengying also supports founders through angel investing and startup scouting for Andreessen Horowitz (a16z). Her work sits at the intersection of data, product, and growth—and she's passionate about helping teams turn insights into breakout momentum.

JOE KUMAR is a senior staff data engineer at Meta with over nine years of experience, dedicated to transforming complex data into actionable insights that drive strategic decision-making. Throughout his career at Meta, Joe has authored a comprehensive playbook for product analytics, empowering product teams to apply best-practice methodologies that enhance their decision-making processes. His commitment to mentorship is evident through the course he teaches as part of the bootcamp onboarding for new data scientists and engineers, ensuring they are equipped with foundational analytical skills.

Joe's expertise also extends to growth analytics, where he has standardized critical concepts and developed a widely adopted playbook for evaluating product market fit. This playbook has been pivotal for major Meta products such as Reels, Threads, and Horizon, helping them refine growth strategies and enhance user engagement. In addition, he created a growth analytics starter kit, a vital resource that simplifies the setup of essential data artifacts for growth analysis across various teams.

With a career marked by innovation, thought leadership, and a relentless pursuit of data-driven excellence, Joe continues to shape the analytical landscape at Meta, driving product growth and strategic success.

YUZHENG SUN, PHD, is a staff data scientist at Statsig.com. He drives best practices in product growth and experimentation, drawing on experience from Tencent, Meta, and Amazon. With over three hundred thousand online followers and over two hundred prominent podcast guests, Yuzheng stands out as a leading voice in data and growth.

A NOTE FROM THE AUTHORS

We welcome your feedback, questions, and success stories as you apply the concepts from this playbook. The growth analytics community thrives on shared learning and collaborative problem-solving. As you implement these frameworks and methodologies, your experiences will contribute to the collective knowledge that pushes the field forward.

www.ingramcontent.com/pod-product-compliance
Lightning Source LLC
Chambersburg PA
CBHW031846200326
41597CB00012B/287